ON BORROWED TIME

GREGOR CRAIGIE

ON BORROWED TIME

North America's
Next Big Quake

Edited by Jill Ainsley.
Cover and page design by Julie Scriver.
Cover images: copyright varunyucg, 123rf.com (graphic); Pixabay (photograph).
Map by Marcel Morin, Lost Art Cartography.
Printed in Canada by Marquis.
10 9 8 7 6 5 4 3 2 1

Library and Archives Canada Cataloguing in Publication

Title: On borrowed time : North America's next big quake / Gregor Craigie.
Names: Craigie, Gregor, author.
Description: Includes bibliographical references.
Identifiers: Canadiana (print) 20210183845 | Canadiana (ebook) 20210183861 | ISBN 9781773102061 (softcover) | ISBN 9781773102078 (EPUB)
Subjects: LCSH: Emergency management—Canada. | LCSH: Emergency management—United States. | LCSH: Natural disasters—Canada. | LCSH: Natural disasters—United States. | LCSH: Earthquake prediction—Canada. | LCSH: Earthquake prediction—United States.
Classification: LCC HV551.5.C3 C73 2021 | DDC 363.340971—dc23

Goose Lane Editions acknowledges the generous support of the Government of Canada, the Canada Council for the Arts, and the Government of New Brunswick.

Goose Lane Editions
500 Beaverbrook Court, Suite 330
Fredericton, New Brunswick
CANADA E3B 5X4
gooselane.com

For my mother, Betty, and my sister, Gillian.

Contents

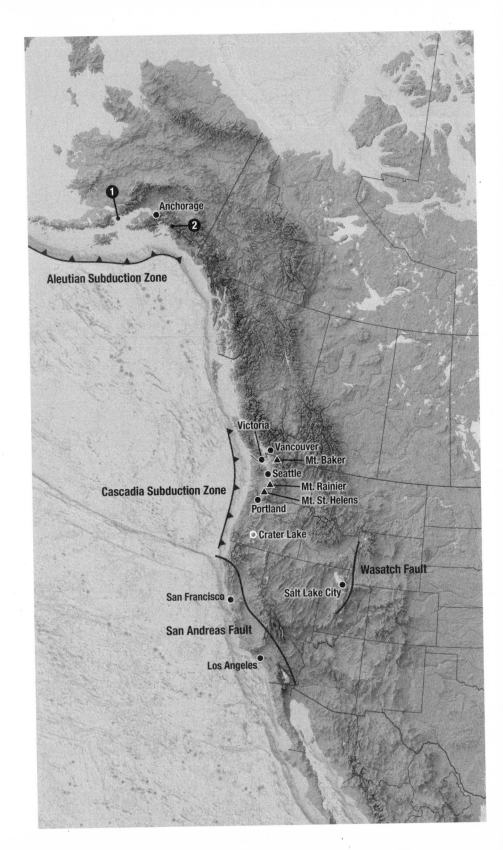

Aleutian Subduction Zone

Anchorage

①

②

Victoria

Vancouver

Mt. Baker

Seattle

Cascadia Subduction Zone

Mt. Rainier

Mt. St. Helens

Portland

Crater Lake

Wasatch Fault

San Francisco

Salt Lake City

San Andreas Fault

Los Angeles

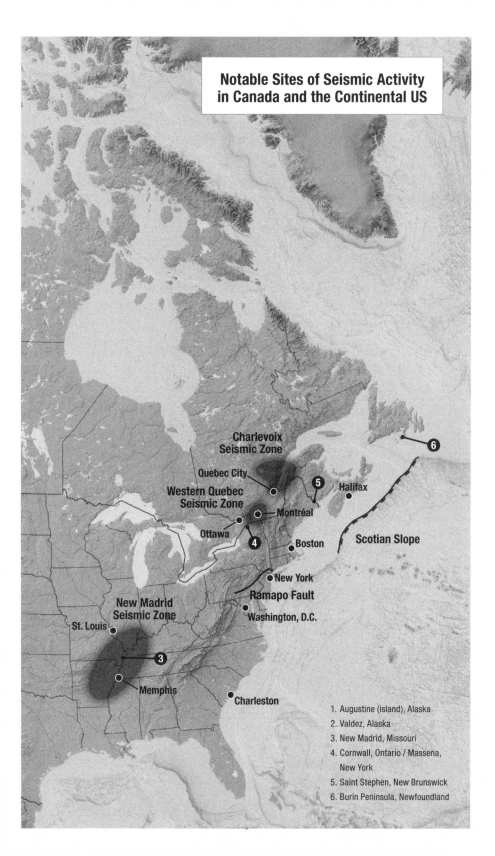

Notable Sites of Seismic Activity in Canada and the Continental US

Charlevoix Seismic Zone

Quebec City

Western Quebec Seismic Zone

Halifax

Montréal

Ottawa

Boston

Scotian Slope

New York

New Madrid Seismic Zone

Ramapo Fault

St. Louis

Washington, D.C.

Memphis

Charleston

1. Augustine (island), Alaska
2. Valdez, Alaska
3. New Madrid, Missouri
4. Cornwall, Ontario / Massena, New York
5. Saint Stephen, New Brunswick
6. Burin Peninsula, Newfoundland

A Quick Word on Magnitude

The first thing most people ask after an earthquake is: how big was it? Earthquakes are difficult to quantify because there are different ways to measure them. Is it the actual force of the ground shaking under a city, or the overall energy expended in a quake? Although many people are familiar with the Richter scale, in this book I use the moment magnitude scale, which the Japanese seismologist Hiroo Kanamori and the American seismologist Thomas C. Hanks developed in the 1970s. The Richter scale and others, like the modified Mercalli intensity scale, work well for describing many seismic events, but the moment magnitude scale is better suited to measuring the world's largest earthquakes.

Introduction

CHRISTCHURCH AND WHAT IT MEANS
FOR NORTH AMERICA

The quake struck in the noon hour, when many office workers in Christchurch's central business district were out looking for lunch. As earthquakes go, the February 2011 temblor was a relatively moderate magnitude-6.3 event, but that number hid the true terror. Accelerometers near the epicentre measured the peak ground acceleration at more than 2g, or twice the force of gravity. That's roughly four times the peak ground force acceleration recorded in the devastating 2010 earthquake in Haiti and roughly twenty times stronger than the force a passenger in a typical commercial airliner might feel during takeoff. The strain on buildings was immense, akin to lifting a hotel or office tower up off the ground and slamming it back down. The peak ground acceleration measurements collected in Christchurch that day were some of the strongest ever recorded, both because the city was so close to the epicentre and because the quake itself was so close to the surface. While the shaking didn't last long, roughly ten seconds, it was severe. Ten seconds was time enough to tear New Zealand's second-largest city apart.

Witnesses reported cars being thrown straight up into the air. The horizontal force was intense, but the vertical motion was even stronger. As stunned city residents would discover seconds later, it was simply too much for some buildings.

More than two hundred people were inside the six-storey Canterbury Television building at the time, which was a relatively modern structure built in the 1980s. The offices and studios of CTV occupied the ground and second floors, the third floor was empty, and different tenants filled the top three storeys, including King's Education, an English-language school, on the fourth floor, a medical clinic on the fifth, and a counselling service on the sixth.

A few minutes before the shaking started, Kendyll Mitchell wrangled her two young children into the elevator. Her eleven-month-old daughter, Ditta, was strapped into a stroller, and her three-year-old son, Jett, was walking beside her. They stepped out of the elevator on the top floor, a few minutes early for a one o'clock counselling appointment. An even larger earthquake had rocked New Zealand's South Island five months earlier. Because it was centred forty kilometres west of the city, the shaking was less intense in Christchurch, but it had terrified Jett. Aftershock after aftershock shook the family's house like a freight train, and the little boy couldn't cope. Kendyll Mitchell was bringing him to see a counsellor for help that afternoon.

Down on the main floor, Maryanne Jackson sat alert at the CTV reception desk. She'd been worried about the building since the quake five months earlier. Although the building had been inspected afterwards, visible cracks later emerged in some walls, and Jackson was worried it might collapse if the ground shook again. Her colleagues had become accustomed to seeing her sprint outside whenever she felt an aftershock.

Up on the fourth floor, Tamara Cvetanova and five fellow students were eating lunch in the kitchen area of the King's Education language school. The native of Serbia had been a pediatrician before moving to New Zealand a decade earlier and had enrolled at the school as part of her effort to recertify as a doctor in New Zealand.

A few blocks away, Ann Brower was sitting on Red Bus 702 with eight other passengers. A lecturer in environmental policy at Lincoln

University, she was on her way to a meeting and was reading the *Economist* magazine as she travelled.

The earthquake started at 12:51 with a powerful upward thrust. At the CTV reception desk, Maryanne Jackson waited a few seconds, then ran for the exit, feeling like the building was chasing after her. By the time she reached the other side of the street, the six-storey structure had pancaked into a dust-shrouded mound of rubble. Only the north shear wall and the elevator shaft stood.

Kendyll Mitchell's infant daughter was still strapped into the stroller when the shaking started. All Mitchell could do was grab the stroller and wrap her arm around her son as the building started to collapse beneath them. The interior wall in front of them fell away from the ceiling, and a glimpse of daylight suddenly appeared through a crack above. Mitchell then felt the sensation of being sucked downward as the floor dropped rapidly. She clutched her children and hung on until falling debris knocked her unconscious.

People outside watched in horror as the CTV building twisted and lurched in multiple directions. The windows exploded in unison as the concrete columns on the fifth floor collapsed and floor after floor plummeted to the ground. Witness estimates of time can be unreliable, but investigators concluded the tragic chain reaction was over less than twenty seconds after the shaking started.

Many of the more than two hundred people who were inside the building were crushed almost instantly, but some survived the collapse. When Kendyll Mitchell regained consciousness, she saw Jett holding her hand and Dita still very much alive in the stroller. Jett was covered in blood, which Mitchell quickly realized was coming from a wound in her head. She'd also suffered a large gash to her leg and a triple fracture to her pelvis. But she was alive, and her children were, too. The three were protected inside a small hole roughly one metre high by one metre wide. A steel beam directly above them protected them from a fatal blow. They were now entombed in a tangle of shattered glass, broken concrete, and bats of pink insulation. Mitchell wiggled her foot out of the rubble but soon realized the broken bits of building above her were just too heavy to move. The elation she felt at surviving the building's collapse was soon eclipsed by the smell of smoke. Would she survive an earthquake only to die in the fire that followed?

Outside the wreckage, stunned survivors stood on the street, trying to come to grips with the scene in front of them. In spite of the shock, a spontaneous army of bystanders burst into action, climbing among the wreckage, searching for anyone who might have survived the building's collapse.

Evan McLellan was working as a plasterer at the nearby St. Paul's Trinity Pacific Presbyterian Church and was still eating lunch when the shaking started. He saw the CTV building go down and ran to the wreckage as soon as the dust cleared. McLellan was one of several who formed a human chain to help survivors down the pile of rubble. But when the trickle of shocked people stumbling out of the wreckage stopped, he worried others might still be trapped inside. "The cops told me to stay put," he told the *New Zealand Herald*, "but I knew time was precious so I did a runner. Something told me to go round the corner of the building, where all the smoke was coming from." McLellan scrambled across mangled beams and broken slabs of concrete, steeling himself for the shock of seeing dead bodies. Instead he heard a woman calling out for help. McLellan followed the voice until he found Kendyll Mitchell and her two children. He started picking through the wreckage until he could see them. He reached down and lifted the two children out first, handing them off to another brave searcher, a man in a button-down shirt and tie, before going back for Kendyll.

Many of the victims of the CTV building collapse had no hope of survival. As is the case in so many earthquakes, human bones are no match for the crushing weight of concrete and steel. Still, rescuers kept picking through the rubble, hoping to pull out the survivors who were buried deeper down. Reaching them was an increasingly difficult task. Police eventually ordered the first rescuers off the rubble in an attempt to prevent even more deaths.

Fire trucks arrived forty minutes after the quake, as the smoke billowing out of the wreckage grew thicker. The firefighters faced a dilemma: the flames were spreading quickly through the debris, but dousing them with a large volume of water might drown trapped survivors. To make matters worse, they had only 1,500 litres of water in the first fire truck, and the earthquake had broken the city's water mains. The volunteers who had moved to the side of the debris pile were put to work listening for survivors' cries for help. Rescuers heard a few trapped people, including a woman who was pinned under a filing cabinet, but others were more difficult to reach.

Rescuers made contact with a group of six students from the language school who were buried under large concrete slabs. Dr. Tamara Cvetanova was one of them. While she was trapped under tonnes of concrete, her husband, Alec Cvetanov, was calling her mobile phone. He could not reach her because the networks were overloaded. Shortly after the quake, Alec left the glass shop where he worked and drove to his children's elementary school. Heavy traffic and shattered roads turned what should have been a twenty-five-minute drive into a four-hour ordeal. Finally, at five o'clock, he left their kids with a neighbour and drove to the CTV building to try to find his wife.

When he arrived, Alec saw rescuers focused on the west side of the building, where they'd made contact with survivors who were still trapped in the kitchen area of the language school. While he watched, he continued to phone his wife, and he finally got through to her at around 11 p.m. Tamara told him her classroom was on the east side of the building and that she was trapped in some sort of tunnel with five classmates. On the east side of the building were large slabs of concrete that would have to be moved by machinery; on the west side were smaller pieces of concrete that could be lifted by hand. Alec told firefighters and the police what his wife had just told him to help them home in on exactly where she and the others were buried. Then he climbed onto the rubble and started banging a piece of concrete. He phoned his wife again, and she told him that she had heard the noise. She could also hear rescuers and the noise of heavy machinery. Then she turned off her phone to conserve the battery. But the heavy-digger operators faced a similar dilemma as the firefighters: lifting an enormous piece of concrete or steel from the top of the pile might allow rescuers to pull someone out alive, but it could also disturb the rubble below and crush someone trapped underneath. Moving massive slabs of concrete could even stoke the fire by providing more oxygen. Sometime in the hours that followed Tamara's final conversation with Alec, she died in the rubble, along with the five fellow students—all of them young nurses who were also studying English—who were near her. Some died of smoke inhalation, while others, including Tamara, were crushed. The coroner could not determine if the heavy machinery or aftershocks had dislodged the debris.

Nineteen medical staff and clinic patients on the fifth floor died, as did seventy students, five teachers, and four staff members of the language school on the fourth floor. And on the bottom two floors, all sixteen of the CTV employees who were inside at the time were killed. Only Maryanne Jackson, who ran from the reception desk, survived. If Kendyll Mitchell and her children were incredibly unlucky to be in the CTV building at the time of the quake, they were at least relatively fortunate to be on the top floor. Of the nineteen people on the sixth floor at the time of the quake, only one was killed.

These were not the only fatalities. Falling bricks and other masonry struck and killed forty-two people in Christchurch that day, including ten people walking on sidewalks. Four pedestrians and eight passengers were crushed when a flurry of rubble from a collapsing brick building rained down on top of the number 702 bus. One moment Ann Brower was reading her magazine, the next she was compressed into a bus seat. Walls of brick crashed onto the roof, forcing it down on the passengers. Brower was pinned, conscious until she passed out from the debilitating pain of a broken pelvis.

Any major earthquake is a shock to the local population, but the Christchurch quake was especially jarring to New Zealand because the country had developed a relatively strong building code and had long prided itself on its seismic readiness. The failure of modern structures like the CTV building shook the nation's confidence. Six days after the quake, Prime Minister John Key announced the government would establish a Royal Commission of Inquiry.

The commission concluded the CTV building collapse was the result of a series of tragic events that started when the local government issued a building permit in the 1980s that didn't meet the seismic standards of the time. It also concluded the engineers in charge of construction lacked the proper experience and oversight. One engineer for the local council had been concerned that the building was not strong enough, but, he told the inquiry, the proponents eventually convinced him it was safe. Seismic weakness was once again identified when the building was sold in 1990, and a number of structural alterations were made, but they might have made the building *more* vulnerable. The concrete columns supporting the floors did not have enough steel reinforcing bar coiled up inside to withstand the force of a major quake, and the concrete surfaces where those columns met the beams were left smooth rather than rough, which led to weaker bonds in those key junctions. To make matters worse, steel reinforcing brackets were attached to exterior walls improperly.

Finally, the building wasn't properly inspected after the September 2010 quake. A team of three people, including one professional engineer, made a quick inspection of the site the day after the quake to check for obvious signs of concern. They found none, and a follow-up inspection carried out two days later, without a professional engineer in attendance, concluded there was no serious threat to the building. Employees were allowed to return to work. The building manager hired a structural engineer to make another inspection but could not provide him with any structural drawings, and the local municipal office was too busy cleaning up its own earthquake damage to search its archives. The families of the 115 people who died in that doomed structure can only wonder if the engineer would have noticed the building's seismic shortcomings if he'd seen those plans.

Though the collapse of a modern structure like the CTV building was shocking, the failure of old brick buildings that day was tragically predictable. Unreinforced masonry buildings, or URMs as they're known to engineers, are extremely vulnerable. Bricks or concrete blocks that are held together with little more than old mortar can withstand the vertical force of gravity for centuries, but they're usually the first structures to fall over when the ground beneath them starts shaking side to side. To make matters worse, the walls are often not fastened securely to the floor joists.

The masonry that fell on Ann Brower's bus could have been secured to the building before the tragedy. In fact, the owner of one of the four addresses that comprised that building had done exactly that following the 2010 earthquake, spending $180,000 to secure the brick parapets to the roof. But the owner of the other three addresses did not. The part of the building that had been fixed lost only a few bricks, which fell onto another bus but caused no deaths or serious injuries. Ann Brower concluded that the other passengers on the 702 bus might have survived "if anyone had the courage to require tie-backs, not just encourage them."

Of course a lot of buildings remained standing, but more than one thousand had to be torn down in the months that followed, and the damage they sustained crippled the local economy. The nineteen-storey Forsythe Barr Building withstood the shaking, but the building's stairwell collapsed, stranding many occupants. An experienced mountain climber inside the building was eventually able to secure a rope and help people rappel out the window to the roof of a neighbouring parking garage. Converted to a hotel and now called the Crowne Plaza, the Forsythe Barr Building is one of the few tall buildings remaining in downtown Christchurch. A shear wall that supported about one-eighth of the twenty-storey Hotel Grand Chancellor's weight failed, and the building leaned ominously, seriously constraining rescue efforts in the area. It was eventually stabilized and dismantled months after the quake.

The combination of strong shaking and weak buildings proved fatal across Christchurch, but there was another deadly factor. The city lies on top of deep alluvial soils, with the top twenty metres under the central business district composed mostly of sand, silt, and peat. A building that stands on soft soils can experience more than double the shaking of a nearby structure that stands on bedrock. But engineering is key. It is almost a cliché among seismologists and engineers: earthquakes don't kill people, buildings kill people. The specific elements of a building's design can make all the difference between life and death. The earthquake is the trigger, but the bullet is the building that falls down and crushes anyone unfortunate enough to be inside. This simple truth helps explain why earthquakes in poorly built cities can kill so many more people than similar seismic events in affluent cities. When a magnitude-7 struck Haiti, thirteen months before the Christchurch quake, the loss of life was apocalyptic. Estimates vary greatly because not all deaths were recorded and others died after the fact from related injuries or diseases like cholera, but the Haitian government estimated 230,000 people were killed. While the overall magnitude of the Christchurch quake was similar in size to the Haiti tremor, it claimed only 185 lives.

The death toll was so much smaller in New Zealand that it's tempting to conclude that developed countries are adequately prepared for major earthquakes, and that concerns about how they will fare seem minor compared to those of the developing world.

But the New Zealand disaster proved the death toll doesn't tell the whole story; even developed cities with modern building codes are extremely vulnerable. The earthquake will have an impact on Christchurch for decades. The central business district was nearly flattened, and infrastructure like roads and utilities were destroyed. Financial losses and psychological trauma prompted thousands of people to leave the city for good. Christchurch is an ominous warning for North American cities like Victoria, BC.

When I first moved to British Columbia's capital city in 2003, I found its many similarities to Christchurch, which I'd visited as a student in the 1990s, striking. Though the two cities are nearly twelve thousand kilometres apart, they bear a striking resemblance to each other. At least, they did before 2011. Both cities were established by the British in the mid-nineteenth century, share similar architecture, and are roughly the same size. But the two cities also share a less pleasant trait: they both stand in active seismic zones that have the potential to wreak havoc.

I first moved to this city to work as a legislative reporter inside the beautiful British Columbia Parliament Buildings. Engineers have assessed the legislature and deemed it especially vulnerable in a major quake. Once the shaking starts, its giant dome could come crashing down and its thick stone walls could collapse, burying hundreds of people inside. But the only politicians who ever talked publicly about fixing the building were the ones I asked directly. And all of them, no matter their political affiliation, seemed to speak from the same script: it would not be acceptable, they repeated, to fix this building when so many schools and other public structures remain vulnerable. To date, no plan to seismically retrofit the irreplaceable British Columbia legislature exists. The politicians aren't the only ones who shrug their shoulders when I mention buildings that might collapse. Many of my friends who grew up here see little point in worrying about something that may not happen until after they're dead.

But Christchurch was a wake-up call for cities on the west coast of North America. Emergency planners in Los Angeles, San Francisco, Portland, Seattle, and Vancouver saw troubling similarities between Christchurch and their own cities. Communities as far-flung as Montréal and Memphis should also be concerned. In fact, the list of seismically vulnerable cities in North America is a long one that includes Charleston, Ottawa, Quebec City, St. Louis, and Salt Lake City. Even New York City is at risk.

Thousands of deaths, millions of people at risk, billions of dollars in potential damage: the numbers associated with earthquakes are overwhelming. For many of us who live in a seismic zone, the initial reaction is shock or surprise at the potential devastation. But that often gives way to a form of devastation fatigue. Not knowing what to do or think, we simply stop thinking about the risk at all.

My interest in earthquakes precedes my move to Victoria. I've been thinking about them ever since I first arrived in Vancouver in the 1990s, largely because I'm a journalist who's interviewed many quake survivors, scientists, and engineers. I've also had a close look at a lot of the innovation: watching engineers shake buildings, ducking under desks with school kids, and squeezing my lanky six-foot-five frame inside North America's first tsunami-survival capsule. So the interest has been professional. But it's also personal. As interesting as the scientific and engineering challenges are, what really fascinates me is our response to the risk — or, in many cases, our lack of response. I suspect millions of us are largely indifferent because we've never lived through a deadly earthquake and don't know what it's like. To be clear, I've never been in a major earthquake. But when I was twelve years old, my family was in a car crash that killed my dad and nearly paralyzed my sister. I've never forgotten the catastrophe that came without warning and shattered my family in seconds. I get a similar sense from every survivor of deadly earthquakes I've ever interviewed — they never saw it coming and can never forget it.

Jim Reimer, a pastor from Nelson, BC, was in Haiti in 2010. "The floor literally lifted up about three feet into the air and threw me across the floor," he says. "It just threw me!" The horror of mangled bodies piled up after the quake traumatized Jim deeply. "I thought I should be pastoring, but I didn't have it in me. I was broken." Jim rallied and has since helped raise hundreds of thousands of dollars for Haitians. But along with a heavy heart for the victims, he's been left with a deep sense of anxiety that whatever building he enters might collapse. "I go into a building and the first thing I do is look for an exit."

Haley Westra was eighteen when she flew to Nepal on a volunteer school-building project—and landed in a giant earthquake. "You'd look over to your left, and there's a building coming down on a family, and you'd look over to your right, and people are just running away from the buildings. And there's screaming and chaos, and you're just frozen." Thousands were buried and millions left homeless in the Himalayan kingdom. The aftershocks continued, but Haley stayed and helped the people of a small mountain village rebuild. When she returned to Victoria, she tripped in the airport a few times because she wasn't accustomed to the ground under her feet remaining still. Haley went on to study nursing, and now she wonders if her hometown is prepared. Apart from physical infrastructure, she questions if we'll have adequate mental health resources. "It's a trauma, so people will need emotional support and psychological support for what they've seen, and the fact that you cannot trust the ground," she says. "I don't trust the ground I walk on anymore."

On a sunny summer day in 2017, I received a copy of a comprehensive seismic report commissioned by the City of Victoria—a thorough examination of the building stock in British Columbia's capital city. The city had released only a brief summary, and I had to submit a freedom-of-information request to see the full report. Reading its dire predictions made for a depressing end to my workday. The study considered several different scenarios, and in the worst crustal and subduction earthquake scenarios, the damage it predicted was staggering: two out of every three buildings in the city of Victoria could either collapse or face demolition. How many thousands of people would be killed or seriously injured in those buildings? The engineers who conducted the study did not answer that question.

After work, I rode my bike up to Government House, the official residence of the lieutenant-governor, the queen's representative in British Columbia. I stood on top of one of the rocky outcrops at the back of the mansion and looked out over the leafy neighbourhood of Fairfield at the bottom of the hill. The view was magnificent, but with that seismic study in mind, I looked down on the bucolic setting and imagined future catastrophe in its place. I saw the first school my oldest son attended, the stores I shop at, and the houses of many friends. These are the homes of teachers, doctors, police officers, firefighters, professors, scientists, journalists, managers, ministers, and midwives. What will happen to our city if two out of every three of us are left homeless in a single day? What will happen if many of us die and even more are injured?

"If you're going to worry about earthquakes," one person told me, "you should probably just move somewhere else."

For many people who live in an active seismic zone, that looks like the only real choice: leave, or refuse to think about it. But a growing number of people have been thinking about earthquakes in recent years; they have discovered that there are other choices, and we can reduce the risk. Not long ago, the mayor of Christchurch travelled to Seattle to speak to local emergency officials. Lianne Dalziel also went for a stroll around the Pioneer Square neighbourhood. She walked among the old brick buildings that date back to the 1800s and are now home to bars, coffee shops, and galleries.

Like many visitors, she admired the eclectic mix of businesses and charming old architecture. But, Dalziel told the *Seattle Times*, she was also reminded of what central Christchurch looked like before it all fell apart, and what happened when it did. The visiting mayor warned Seattle to guard against a similar fate: "You might be on borrowed time."

ONE

The West Coast

Chapter 1

UNEARTHING THE RISK IN CASCADIA

When George Vancouver sailed to the west coast of North America in 1792, he spent months surveying the meandering inlets and channels of what we now call the Salish Sea. The British captain bestowed English names as he explored, from the Gulf of Georgia down to Puget Sound. The temperate corner of the planet enchanted him. "The serenity of the climate, the innumerable pleasing landscapes, and the abundant fertility that unassisted nature puts forth," he wrote, "require only to be enriched by the industry of man."

It took several decades for European settlers to follow in any serious numbers. When they did, many found the long stretch of coastline from northern California up to the Alaska Panhandle, which some now call Cascadia, similarly beguiling. And who could blame them? Cascadia was heaven on Earth. Salmon in their millions swam up great rivers. Vast temperate rainforests of ancient cedar, fir, and hemlock stretched skyward and blanketed the mountainous terrain. And then there was the climate, so much more forgiving and hospitable than in the harsh continental expanse on the other side of the coastal mountains.

First Nations had lived here and thrived for thousands of years before Europeans arrived. They knew more about the land than most newcomers gave them credit for, and although they told tales of great tremors and terrifying ocean waves that followed, almost none of the settlers listened. Nor did they see any obvious signs of great upheaval in the earth: the rapid regrowth of plant life over rock and the long silences between shaking left no conspicuous physical markers of past calamities.

That perception of Cascadia as a benevolent paradise persisted through the nineteenth century and well into the early twentieth. Even after the devastating San Francisco earthquake of 1906, the presumption that Cascadia was just out of harm's way endured. Victoria had become home to the first seismograph in the region in 1899, and some wanted to make the provincial capital known as a front-row seat to one of the world's greatest spectacles. In a 1911 editorial urging Canada's federal government to establish a seismological observatory in Victoria, the *Daily Colonist* newspaper proclaimed the city "admirably situated" as a location for seismic observation. "It is near one of the world's great lines of weakness, and yet just far enough away to be without the danger zone. We occasionally get the tail end of an earthquake here, and while it is not sufficient to cause alarm it is possible to have it well recorded on the local seismograph." In Seattle in the 1920s, a University of North Carolina geologist named Collier Cobb assured members of the local chamber of commerce that the deep glacial drift beneath Seattle gave it a natural "shock absorber which makes the city immune from disaster from quakes."

Some geologists went so far as to predict the risk of earthquakes would decline everywhere. "Geology teaches that these great natural forces are waning," Professor Hugh Sherwood wrote in a 1906 US Weather Bureau report. "Such manifestations are dying out as the crust becomes thicker and more solid and settled. We are not on the eve of renewed and widespread earthquake and volcanic activity, as some would lead us to believe, but rather are living in the last days of such phenomena."

Geologists who expected earthquakes to continue as they always had made no mention of a special threat to British Columbia or the Pacific Northwest. Hours of combing through digital archives of early-twentieth-century newspapers produces several reports of modest earthquakes but only one story that even raised the possibility of a major quake. The article appeared in the *Evening Statesman* in Walla Walla, Washington, a few weeks after the San Francisco quake. "Woman Declares that Seattle Will Be Next," the headline bellowed. "Seattle will be destroyed by an earthquake during the last week of May, according to a prophecy made by Mrs. Margaret Albright of 418 Rainier Avenue, Georgetown. Mrs. Albright says she is a prophetess, and as such she advises all residents of the city to leave before May 27, and take their possessions east of the mountains." Mrs. Albright was not taken seriously. She "informed Bishop O'Dea and other prominent churchmen of what is to come, but complains that they refuse to place any credence in it—in fact, that they ridicule it."

It would be many decades before people in Cascadia took the idea of a truly devastating earthquake seriously. But as the century progressed, occasional earthquakes gave them an uneasy sense that the region might be prone to seismic activity after all. In 1946 a magnitude-7.3 crustal earthquake shook the town of Courtenay on Vancouver Island. Chimneys fell from homes across the region and a thirty-foot tidal wave swept across Comox Lake, considerably damaging a local logging company. But the small population of central Vancouver Island and the relative lack of big buildings meant only two people died. One man drowned when a wave flooded his dinghy, and a frightened sixty-nine-year-old man in Seattle suffered a heart attack. The death toll might have been much higher if the quake had not happened on a Sunday morning, as an elementary school chimney crashed into a classroom that normally sheltered sixty children. The quake still stands as Canada's largest-ever recorded onshore earthquake, but it did little to concern people farther south.

Three years later, a smaller earthquake in Washington had a bigger impact. The 1949 Olympia earthquake was measured at magnitude 6.7. Eight people died, including eleven-year-old Marvin Klegman in Tacoma. Klegman was on duty as a lunchtime crossing guard at Lowell Elementary School and leading a kindergarten student through the front doors when the bricks from a roof cornice cascaded down. Klegman shielded the smaller boy from the bricks, and in doing so saved the life of Kelcy Allen while losing his own. A statue in front of Lowell Elementary depicts the two boys running hand in hand, and April 13 is Marvin Klegman Day in Tacoma. The damage in and around Seattle was considerable, but it would take another sixteen years before the first real cracks in Cascadia's complacence really started to show.

Seven people died in the 1965 Puget Sound quake, and millions of dollars in damage was done to two Boeing factories in the Seattle area that were built on artificial fill and mudflats. The quake had the same magnitude and intensity as the 1949 event, but this time people began thinking seriously about earthquakes in Cascadia. The California Division of Mines and Geology noted with interest how the Puget Sound quake differed from typical California temblors: there were no visible faults on the ground, it was much deeper (forty-eight kilometres below the surface), and it produced no aftershocks. "Every earthquake has unique or unusual features," the report concluded. "Only by well-coordinated, immediate interdisciplinary study of every earthquake along the Pacific margin can we hope to gain that knowledge that will be most useful in minimizing damage and loss of life in future earthquakes."

Scientists from the US Geological Survey, the University of Oregon, and the University of Washington created the Pacific Northwest Seismic Network. Starting with just five seismometers in 1969, the network eventually acquired more than three hundred and is now considered the second largest in the United States. The Pacific Northwest Seismic Network was formed just as scientists were starting to agree on the theory of plate tectonics, which evolved out of the ideas of continental drift and seafloor spreading and offered an explanation for the formation of mountains and volcanoes, and the advent of earthquakes.

Earth's surface is made up of fifteen to twenty tectonic plates, which reach down about one hundred kilometres below the surface and form the earth's hard outer crust. Some scientists compare the plates to pieces of an egg's cracked shell. The plates sit on top of what is believed to be a much hotter and more liquid layer called the asthenosphere. Heat from deep inside keeps the asthenosphere malleable and essentially greases the wheels of the plates above so they can move. As a result, Earth's plates grind and rumble up against each other in sometimes violent outbursts. The slow-moving convection currents in the asthenosphere push hot molten rock known as magma up to the surface through volcanoes and through cracks in the ocean floor, where the plates meet. When two plates move away from each other, the magma seeps up into the gap left behind and solidifies into new oceanic crust. Where two plates push together, the older, denser edges of one plate are pushed under the other and back down into the asthenosphere. Scientists call this subduction, and it is what produces the world's biggest earthquakes.

Subduction zone quakes happen in Cascadia, but this is only a relatively recent discovery. In fact, the idea that offshore megathrust earthquakes happen here was denied in peer-reviewed scientific papers as recently as 1979. Just as it had taken scientists decades to develop the theory of plate tectonics, it would take many years and some remarkable scientific sleuthing to piece together the Cascadia earthquake puzzle.

In the mid-1960s, scientists from Oregon State University collected the first concrete evidence that the ocean floor from northern California up to Vancouver Island can produce huge earthquakes. But they didn't realize the significance of what they had found until much later. Oceanographers took to the water to investigate the 2,200-kilometre-long Cascadia Channel at the bottom of the Pacific in 1965. Not much was known about deep sea channels at the time, so oceanographer Verne Kulm and a team of scientists on the research vessel *Yaquina* lowered thirty-foot-long pistons and plunged them into the ocean floor. The pistons cut out long cylinders, and the ship's crew then winched the two-thousand-pound samples up to the surface and hauled them aboard, often in rough seas in the middle of the night.

"What was immediately apparent when I opened the first cores collected from the channel floor," wrote oceanographer Gary Griggs, "was the rhythmic nature of the sediment sequences." Griggs found thin grey layers of clay up to five centimetres thick alternating with olive-green layers up to three and a half metres thick. The green layers were telltale signs of underwater landslides that had happened over many centuries. Those layers are called turbidites, and the rhythmic nature Griggs wrote about told a story of massive events that repeated themselves over and over again for thousands of years. The pattern of slides was remarkably similar in three separate samples taken along a nearly one-hundred-kilometre stretch of the channel—this suggested these slides were huge, because they happened over such a large area. Scientists used radiocarbon dating to determine the turbidites were less than 12,500 years old, which meant they formed after the last Ice Age. In the thirteenth layer they found 7,700-year-old volcanic ash from the eruption of Mount Mazama, which now holds Crater Lake in Oregon. This showed them that there had been thirteen massive underwater slides since the eruption of Mount Mazama, and that these events occurred every four hundred to six hundred years. But they could not answer the difficult question of what caused the slides. Only two explanations seemed plausible at the time: severe storms or earthquakes. Those core samples went largely forgotten for two decades. But research in other areas was picking up steam.

In the early 1980s, geophysicists demonstrated that the Juan de

Fuca plate, the relatively small crustal plate squeezed between the bigger Pacific and North American plates, was still subducting. In other words, the Juan de Fuca plate was moving roughly an inch a year, or roughly two and half metres per century. That may sound tiny in comparison to an entire continent, but it is similar to other active subduction zones, like the ones off Japan and Chile, where massive earthquakes occur.

Geologist Jim Savage, who led important research in subduction earthquakes in Alaska in the 1960's, turned his attention to Washington State. He studied historical highway surveys and demonstrated the crust was being deformed and that the mountains of the Olympic Peninsula were tilting eastward as that crustal squeeze continued. Although that squeeze wasn't proof of past earthquakes, it was a telltale sign that many of the key characteristics of Cascadia mirrored those of Alaska.

Meanwhile, other scientists were comparing Cascadia to other subduction zones around the Pacific Ocean's infamous Ring of Fire. In 1984 seismologists Tom Heaton and Hiroo Kanamori from the California Institute of Technology published a paper that showed Cascadia shares many traits with Chile, Alaska, and other deadly subduction zones. They noted the oceanic crust in Cascadia is relatively younger and hotter than other oceanic crust and therefore lighter and more buoyant, which means it isn't likely to slide under the continent smoothly. In this and other ways Cascadia looked just like the other subduction zones. The only real difference was that Cascadia lacked a recorded history of catastrophic earthquakes. So scientists went looking.

Much of the research at the time was funded by the nuclear industry, which wanted to build new reactors in Washington State. Before regulators issued permits they wanted to understand the local seismic risk, so they requested several studies to help them. Many established geologists had spent years reassuring people that the Cascadia Subduction Zone could not produce anything bigger than a magnitude-7.5 earthquake. The industry hoped that would be enough to ensure the approval of new reactors, but some seismologists were not willing to rule out bigger quakes. In the end, the nuclear proponents faced bigger problems than the seismic risk, and strong community opposition and financial problems defeated them.

While nuclear proposals fizzled, geological investigation caught fire and sparked new studies and research projects in the lab and the field. In 1986 geologist Brian Atwater of the US Geological Survey went looking for clues in the estuaries of Washington State. Paddling an aluminum canoe up and down muddy streams, he found giant old-growth trees standing dead in swampy tidal flats. These ghost trees had remained upright for centuries in salt water because Western Red Cedar is so good at withstanding rot. The sturdy trees turned out to be critical pieces of the Cascadia puzzle.

Atwater found another key puzzle piece in the mud. He dug up layers of sediment that proved a great surge of sand and sea water had long ago flooded the land. In bay after bay, river mouth after river mouth, Atwater and his research team found the same evidence: buried remains of old forests and marshes that had subsided below sea level to become tidal mudflats. "Some of the soils retain delicate remains of plants that had been living on them at the time of submergence," he wrote. "Tidal-flat mud above such soils entombed herbaceous leaves and stems, in growth position, before they had time to rot." Up until this point, scientists had engaged in a vigorous debate about whether the Cascadia Subduction Zone was capable of massive quakes. But when added to the other research, Atwater's findings gave a huge boost to the argument that Cascadia really does shake.

Then, in 1987, Oregon State University geologist Robert Yeats organized a scientific workshop the night before a meeting of the Oregon Academy of Science. The topic of the meeting was a straightforward question: Is There a Major Earthquake Hazard in

Oregon or Not? Yeats and the other organizers invited a number of key geologists to speak, including Brian Atwater, Tom Heaton, and a young New Zealander named John Adams, who would lead critical research at the Geological Survey of Canada. Yeats recalls that many of the scientists who had been skeptical attended, but all of them were in agreement when they left: there is an earthquake risk in Cascadia, and it's a big one. "The meeting marked a paradigm change," he wrote, "a fundamental change in our thinking." Right after the meeting, John Adams went to Oregon State University to examine the ocean floor core samples that researchers had hauled up to the surface in the 1960s. With the benefit of twenty more years of research into plate tectonics and an improved understanding of how the Juan de Fuca and North American plates are colliding, Adams published an article arguing that the turbidites collected from the Pacific Ocean floor amounted to a geological record of massive earthquakes in the past.

Meanwhile, Brian Atwater and his research team were gathering more evidence of past tsunamis. Atwater enlisted the help of David Yamaguchi, a dendrochronologist (tree-ring expert) from the University of Washington. Any log or tree stump has a pattern of thin and thick rings that show the sequence of droughts or strong growth over the tree's life. To dendrochronologists, the rings form a sort of ecological barcode that can help scientists match one tree to another. Yamaguchi examined samples from the ghost trees that Atwater had found and embarked on painstaking counts of their rings to try to determine how old the trees were when they died. He then compared them to the rings of newly cut old-growth trees to learn when those long-dead trees died. Using tree-ring data and radiocarbon dating technology, he was able to determine that the trees died sometime in the late 1600s or early 1700s.

Atwater and Yamaguchi also uncovered evidence that the land itself had dropped suddenly. When Yamaguchi examined the roots of dead Sitka spruce trees they found, he discovered wide outer rings that told a tale of vigorously growing trees that were healthy right up to the time of their death. There was no sign of a prolonged death, such as from gradual saltwater poisoning or drowning, and this indicated a sudden event had killed the trees.

Atwater put this together with the rest of the evidence to show Cascadia had produced a major earthquake roughly three hundred years ago. Still, its size wasn't clear. Could Cascadia shake as much as other subduction zones around the world? Was it capable of rupturing its entire length and triggering a massive magnitude-9 earthquake? To answer this crucial question, scientists went looking for clues in new places.

The rich oral histories of Indigenous peoples included stories from different villages of a great shaking followed by a huge wave that washed many people away. James Swan, an Indian agent and the first schoolteacher at the Makah Reservation in Neah Bay, Washington, kept a detailed diary of his years with the Makah, and in 1864 he recorded a story told to him by Billy Balch, the Makah's leader — a story passed down through several generations. The ocean water, Balch said, rose up in Neah Bay and flooded the Waatch prairie. The water spread across the flat strip of land all the way to the other side of the cape and rejoined the Pacific Ocean a few miles away, effectively turning Cape Flattery into an island. The water then receded from Neah Bay, leaving it dry. After that, the water rose again "without any swell or waves and submerged the whole of the cape and in fact the whole country except the mountains back of Clyoquot," Swan wrote. Balch told Swan that those who managed to jump into their canoes survived. They floated away in the strong current, with some making landfall at Nootka Sound on the northwest coast of Vancouver Island, where their descendants still live. But others drowned in the rapidly rising waters that stranded their canoes high in the trees. "The Waatch prairie shows conclusively that the waters of the ocean once flowed through it," Swan concluded.

The Makah's oral history bore a striking resemblance to tales from other Indigenous groups up and down the coast, from northern California to Vancouver Island. The stories were not written down until the 1860s, nearly fifty years after European settlement began and almost a century after the first European contact. By that time, scholars suggest, most oral traditions were likely lost, because of the large numbers of deaths from introduced diseases like smallpox and the disruption of family life that occurred when children were sent to residential schools. Still, Indigenous people shared stories of a frightening battle between Thunderbird and Whale that involved great shaking and flooding. The Tillamook people in northern Oregon recounted one of their stories to the anthropologist Franz Boas in the 1890s. "The Thunderer told him to stand aside," Boas wrote, "as he himself was preparing to catch whales. He caught the largest one and carried it up to a large cave which was nearby, and when he had deposited it there the whale flapped its tail and jumped about, violently shaking the mountain so that it was impossible to stand upon it."

Many of the Indigenous stories that anthropologists recorded between 1860 and 1964 are general in nature, but nine mention specific events that helped geologists estimate the date of the great earthquake, and some even specified the number of generations that had passed since the stories were first told. When geologist Ruth Ludwin eliminated the earliest and latest dates, she calculated an average midpoint of 1701.

Possibly the clearest Indigenous account of the great Cascadia earthquake was recorded in 1964, shortly after a gigantic earthquake in Alaska sent a tsunami wave surging up the Alberni Inlet on the west coast of Vancouver Island. The late Chief Louis Nookmis of Pachena Bay described a quake that struck many generations earlier. It came at night, he said, and was followed by a deadly wave soon after. "They had practically no way or time to try to save themselves. I think it was at night-time that the land shook.…A big wave smashed into the beach. The Pachena Bay people were lost." The Indigenous history completed a huge portion of the Cascadia Subduction Zone puzzle, but the final pieces came from a surprising location on the other side of the Pacific Ocean.

The word *tsunami* originated in Japan, with the prefix *tsu* translating as harbour and *nami* meaning waves. Japan is sadly familiar with this unique form of natural disaster. Japanese written history includes a long list of tsunamis, with the first one recorded in the year 684 CE. Many tsunamis have washed ashore in Japan over the years since, bringing death and destruction in varying degrees. Most followed great earthquakes that acted as warnings to the people living along the coast to run for higher ground. But written Japanese records also make occasional mention of orphan tsunamis that struck without warning. Orphan tsunamis are caused by massive subduction zone earthquakes that are too far away to be felt where the tsunamis eventually make landfall. The world's biggest subduction earthquakes have claimed victims many thousands of kilometres away, such as the 1960 Chilean earthquake, which generated a tsunami that killed sixty-one people in Hilo, Hawaii, several hours later.

In the 1990s, geologist Kenji Satake at the Geological Survey of Japan heard about Brian Atwater's work and wondered if one of Japan's old orphan tsunamis might be connected to Cascadia. Satake found Japanese records of an orphan tsunami in the year 1700. It affected six towns and villages along a nine-hundred-kilometre stretch of coast on the main island of Honshu and did not correspond to earthquakes known to have occurred in South America, Alaska, or Kamchatka. Some samurai wrote detailed reports of a rising sea that came without warning in the middle of a winter night in late January 1700. The wave was recorded simultaneously in the villages of Kuwagasaki and Otsuchi, thirty kilometres to the south. Kuwagasaki lost thirty of its three hundred houses to tsunami waves up to five metres high and to fires that broke out afterwards. Villagers ran for high ground, and a request for help was sent to the nearby town of Miyako.

Knowing both the time the orphan tsunami struck and the angle at which it washed ashore led researchers to conclude it came from Cascadia and had started at roughly 9 p.m. local time on January 26, 1700. Scientists calculated that a wave large enough to reach Japan with such force would have sped across the Pacific Ocean for roughly ten hours before making landfall and must have been from a magnitude-9 or greater quake. Geologists could now fit the Japanese puzzle pieces into the picture and see the Cascadia Subduction Zone for what it really is: a massive undersea fault that has produced some of the world's biggest earthquakes—and will do so again.

As if a megathrust monster lurking offshore isn't bad enough, the Pacific Northwest and British Columbia have to worry about two other types of earthquake: deep intraslab quakes, and shallow crustal quakes.

While most earthquakes take place along the plate boundaries, an intraslab event rumbles up from the deep interior of a plate. The three most damaging quakes to hit Washington State in the last century were all intraslab earthquakes that started a long way down, where the Juan de Fuca plate dips below the continental North American plate. The 1949 and 1965 temblors were intraslab quakes, and the 2001 Nisqually quake rumbled up from fifty-five kilometres below the waters of the Nisqually Delta. The 6.8-magnitude quake caused severe shaking and injured four hundred people. No deaths were attributed to the quake itself, though one person reportedly died from a heart attack. The quake damaged the air traffic control tower at Sea-Tac Airport and the dome on the Capitol in Olympia.

Intraslab earthquakes have the potential to cause serious damage in and around Seattle, in particular, and many old brick buildings in downtown Seattle were damaged. But it's crustal earthquakes that could be the most devastating if they strike near a major city. Crustal earthquakes occur closer to the surface, typically at depths of less than thirty kilometres. In the Cascadia region, these crustal quakes happen in the continental North American plate. The size depends on the length of the fault, but some faults in the Puget Sound region and southern Vancouver Island could unleash horrific damage.

The Seattle fault is of particular concern. More of a fault zone than a single fault, this connection of shallow thrust faults could produce an earthquake of up to magnitude 7 in, frighteningly, the middle of a metropolitan area. It runs right under Lumen Field, home to the Seattle Seahawks and up to sixty-eight thousand deafening fans every game day. Fortunately, the stadium was engineered with this quake in mind. But a long list of nearby structures were not. If a magnitude-6.3 tremor under Christchurch could do that much damage, what would a magnitude-7 monster under a metropolis with more than ten times the population do?

Scientists believe the Seattle fault last ruptured about 1,100 years ago. One of the first clues was found more than a century ago, just east of Seattle, deep in the waters of Lake Washington. Early settlers noticed well-preserved old-growth trees submerged deep in the lake. Some guessed the trees had long ago plunged into the water in a massive landslide. One hundred seventy-five of the trees were removed to allow for navigation in 1919, but others were left in the murky depths. In the early 1990s, scientists recovered some of the trees still in the lake and used radiocarbon dating to establish they had indeed been part of a landslide roughly one thousand years ago. They also found evidence of rock slides on the Olympic Peninsula, dating from the same event, and of a localized tsunami that swept up Puget Sound, all pointing to a major earthquake of roughly magnitude 7. "Were this earthquake to repeat today," geologist Robert Yeats wrote, "the losses would be catastrophic." A 2002 study concluded a shallow magnitude-7 event would damage hundreds of old buildings and eighty bridges, many more than in an offshore magnitude-9 megathrust earthquake.

A similar threat lies in wait close to Victoria. The Devil's Mountain fault stretches from the foothills of Washington State's Cascade mountain range, down under the waters of the Juan de Fuca Strait, to the western suburbs of Victoria, where it joins the Leech River fault system. Until recently, scientists believed the Leech River fault had been inactive for millions of years. But field geologist Kristen Morrell at the University of Victoria demonstrated the fault has ruptured three times in the last twelve thousand years. The most recent event was 1,600 years ago and may have coincided with a massive offshore rupture of the Cascadia Subduction Zone.

The scenario of what would essentially be a double earthquake is a terrifying one for emergency planners to imagine. At a technical lunch in 2017, Morrell chose her words carefully and stressed several times that the information should spur people to prepare, not panic. Other, as yet unknown, faults lie beneath the forests of Vancouver Island, Morrell said, and those unknown faults can change communities forever. She pointed to the Christchurch quake as evidence that relatively small faults can still be deadly if they are close to cities. "If they're right beneath the population centre and we don't have any information of it being there, it can be destructive," she warned.

While the extent of the seismic risk in some of our cities is relatively new, knowledge of the risk old brick buildings pose is not. Municipal leaders in Seattle first tried to compel owners to strengthen their old brick buildings in the 1970s. Not surprisingly, the owners balked at the cost, and half a century later the issue is still debated. In the meantime more than one thousand buildings remain vulnerable, and more than thirty thousand people live, work, or study inside them. Some buildings in Seattle have been retrofitted over the years, but many more remain untouched, their owners either ignoring the risk entirely or choosing to put it off for another day.

"The one thing I'd say is missing is a sense of urgency," Eric Holdeman sighs. Holdeman has spent thirty years trying to spark that sense of urgency, as a manager in state government, the emergency management director for King County, and security director for the Port of Tacoma. Called "our John the Baptist" by a colleague, Holdeman is well known around Seattle for his zeal in preaching the need to prepare. He's also grown accustomed to many of the people around him simply shrugging off the risk. He predicts it will take "a really good shaker where one bridge falls down and one building collapses and nobody dies" to motivate people.

If Washington State does not make major improvements before either the Seattle fault or the Cascadia Subduction Zone rumble again, Holdeman foresees a calamity as bad as, or worse than, what New Orleans suffered in Hurricane Katrina in 2005, when seven hundred people were killed and hundreds of thousands of people had to leave the city. "I believe absolutely there will be a spontaneous evacuation of Seattle after about two days," Holdeman says. "No one should be saying aid is coming. It'll take too long, and people start dying after seventy-two hours without water, so they'll be drinking dirty water. And this is the generation that does not have a pantry, so they'll have to walk out and leave."

Despite that dismal prediction, Holdeman is quick to point out that the vast majority of people will survive, suggesting only about 2 percent of the population will perish, even in a catastrophic earthquake. But that would amount to thousands of deaths, and Holdeman says many of them will be in the rubble of Seattle's unreinforced masonry buildings. "If your spouse or significant other or friend works in a URM building, my recommendation is that they buy more life insurance because those guys have a much higher likelihood of dying."

Three hours down the interstate, Portland faces a similar risk. Though smaller than Seattle, Portland actually has more vulnerable brick buildings. In fact, it may have the highest number on the West Coast. In a soberingly detailed online database, the City of Portland lists more than 1,600 unreinforced masonry buildings that could collapse in a major earthquake. Offices, auditoriums, schools, colleges, churches, garages, restaurants, cafés, doughnut shops, warehouses, and apartments are located inside these potentially lethal structures. Some are squat one-storey affairs, but most are multi-level buildings, with a few rising up to eight storeys. Roughly seven thousand residential units are housed in them.

Like Seattle, Portland has struggled to come up with an effective plan that addresses this significant risk to public safety. In 1995 the city introduced a bylaw that required old brick buildings to undergo a seismic retrofit if more than 50 percent of the roof was replaced, but many building owners responded by replacing 49 percent of the roof and waiting to repair the rest. Two decades later, only a fifth of the buildings identified in the mid-nineties had been retrofitted, so the city made another effort to make private buildings safer. In 2018, city commissioners debated a new mandate that would require all owners to perform retrofits within ten or fifteen years. To many, it was a simple and sensible solution, given the thousands of people who could be crushed inside these structures. But with repair bills typically running from hundreds of thousands of dollars into the millions for a single building, many owners complained about the expense and once again avoided being forced to act.

Vancouver, BC, has also delayed for decades. A report prepared for the city in 1993 identified 1,100 unreinforced masonry buildings at risk of collapse. But twenty-five years later, the city had not come up with a comprehensive strategy to retrofit the buildings to withstand a major earthquake. Some of those vulnerable buildings were demolished to make way for glitzy new condo towers. Others were retrofitted because the building owners wanted to renovate and were required to perform seismic upgrades to receive building permits. Still, hundreds remain standing and are just as dangerous today.

Vancouver's Downtown Eastside is one of Canada's poorest neighbourhoods. It's also one of its liveliest. Day and night, residents of tiny single-room occupancy hotel rooms spill out onto the streets: wheeling, dealing, arguing, injecting, dumpster diving, and simply scraping out a living in whatever way they can. The impoverished residents of this neighbourhood would likely be some of the first victims if an earthquake strikes, as many of the old buildings surrounding them would shower bricks down onto the sidewalk below or collapse entirely. And brick buildings aren't the only concern.

Vancouver now has more than seven hundred buildings that are twelve storeys or higher. While Metro Vancouver has nearly 2.5 million people, the city itself has only 750,000 residents. That means the ratio of high-rise buildings to people in Vancouver is roughly one to one thousand, considerably higher than New York City. Vancouver's high-rises give the city a vibrancy and population density that many people love. But these buildings could also pose a serious risk in a big earthquake.

You don't need to go far from the old hotels in the Downtown Eastside before the brick buildings start to intermingle with newer condo towers to the west, and the demographics change accordingly, with fewer people pushing shopping carts and more tucking rolled-up yoga mats under their arms. These new towers should remain standing if a Cascadia Subduction Zone quake sends long rolling waves through the ground, but structural engineers warn some of these buildings may be so heavily damaged that they will have to be torn down.

For many years, the seismic risk of individual buildings and building types in Vancouver was not well studied. That's started to change recently. Engineering professor Perry Adebar at the University of British Columbia led a team of engineers who reviewed the plans of about 350 towers. Towers in Vancouver can be roughly grouped into those that were built before the introduction of seismic building provisions in the building code in 1985, and the ones that were built after. Adebar cautions that age alone is not enough information to deem a building dangerous or safe. He's confident many older towers will withstand big earthquakes, and he also fears some new ones will not. But in general, the older ones are more likely to be at risk.

In many ways, Vancouver is better off than other West Coast cities. Los Angeles has roughly 1,500 vulnerable concrete-frame buildings that can collapse if powerful twisting, or torsional, forces put too much pressure on individual columns. Most of Vancouver's older towers are built with shear walls, which act as strong inner cores, like spines that guard against wind and other lateral forces like earthquakes. The shear walls absorb that force and transfer it down to the building's foundation, thereby preventing the frame from twisting out of joint. That's the good news.

The bad news for Vancouver is that many of those older towers contain what could prove to be critical weaknesses. Some of them have very thin shear walls with only one layer of steel reinforcement and no reinforcement at the edge of the wall. Some have large openings in the walls for windows. And some have walls on upper floors that stand farther away from the centre of the building than the walls below them, which can increase the pressure on the lower floors considerably. Another concern in many old towers is that their floor slabs lack the stronger reinforcements of newer buildings, which tie the floors to the columns that support them. As a result these older floors are more likely to detach from the columns, and some might collapse. "The reality is if we got a really strong earthquake close by that created really strong ground shaking in the city, yes, a few buildings will collapse," Adebar says.

Buildings aren't the only concern. Bridges and freeway infra-structure are also vulnerable. A lot of overpasses in and around

Seattle were built before bridge and overpass requirements in the United States were strengthened in the 1970s, and many still haven't been replaced or retrofitted. Eric Holdeman knows these deficiencies as both an emergency planner and a daily commuter. When he worked as the emergency management director for King County, his thirty-five-mile commute took him over more than twenty bridges that could collapse in a major earthquake, some because of insufficient steel reinforcement in the concrete and others because the roadway wasn't fastened to the concrete columns supporting them. Some might simply sink when the ground beneath them liquefies. Seismic improvements have been carried out on a number of bridges and overpasses over the years, typically on highways that stood on solid ground and therefore had a better chance of withstanding a major quake. Whenever King County's emergency management director contemplated going to work in an emergency, he imagined having to cross several downed bridges. "My plan was to put the bicycle in the back seat, drive as far as I could, then ride. If I couldn't ride, then I'd walk."

There are many other types of vulnerable infrastructure. Pipelines, railways, electrical grids, and fibre-optic communication networks can all be severed. Giant storage tanks and other buoyant structures can float up as the soft soils below them liquefy, and piers and other port infrastructure can be heavily damaged if not completely destroyed. The list of things that could go wrong is dismayingly long. But fortunately for us, the number of people trying to design and build safeguards to protect us when the shaking starts is growing.

Chapter 2
RESPONDING TO THE RISK

The University of British Columbia campus was much quieter than usual. Only a small fraction of the student population was enrolled in summer courses, and the especially hot weather seemed to have sent most of them indoors. But a short stroll away from the calm quiet of the library, a much more vigorous exercise was about to begin in the Earthquake Engineering Research Facility.

The cavernous room resembled an aircraft hangar more than a classroom. At the front door, engineer Graham Taylor welcomed a group of younger engineers who'd come over for the day from Victoria. A native of Australia, Taylor is a veteran of seismic research who's spent decades designing retrofits to make schools, offices, emergency buildings, and houses better able to withstand strong earthquakes. Wearing safety glasses and a red hard hat that covered most of his grey hair, Taylor guided the other engineers around the steel elephant in the room: a giant platform called a shake table. More of a frame than a table, the giant assembly consists of long steel beams bolted together and painted royal blue. On top of the long beams sat a large plywood box the size of a typical public-school classroom. There was an opening for a door and several more for windows but no glass or furniture because the engineers were only interested in assessing the walls and what they might withstand. Those walls were built with standard two-by-six-inch wood studs, plywood nailed on the outside of the studs and drywall on the inside. On top of the flat roof, engineers had used a massive crane to place six giant steel plates; the crane still lurked overhead. Those plates added up to twenty metric tonnes, roughly ten times the weight of the wood structure itself.

In most major earthquakes, a lot of buildings are damaged partially but don't collapse completely. That leads to critical questions. Is it safe to go back inside? How would you know? But post-quake assessments can be difficult to make quickly and correctly. That's why Taylor invited the engineers to the UBC engineering lab. He briefed the engineers on the three shake tests that would be performed that day and explained that after each test they would break into small groups to assess the building for damage.

Everyone stood back as Mehrtash Motamedi, the head laboratory engineer, made a few last-minute adjustments and started the video cameras placed in different spots around the lab. His assistants went back up to the control room to look down at the shake table through a large window. A native of Iran, one of the most seismically active countries in the world, Motamedi has overseen many important structural tests like this one. He grabbed the start button, took a deep breath, and exhaled slowly. He wore a look of intense concentration, reminiscent of an Olympic pole-vaulter just before the start of their run: pole raised, eyes fixed on the bar. The tension in the room inched up as he took one last breath. Then he pressed the start button, and the test began.

A strobe light on the ceiling flashed orange as the shaking started slowly, almost anticlimactically. The engineers had pre-programmed the same wave pattern that was recorded in the 2011 Tohoku earthquake in Japan, a quake that started softly but soon swelled into a seismic storm. That massive subduction zone earthquake produced shaking similar to what the Cascadia Subduction Zone quake will produce, so Taylor thought it would be a useful simulation, "imitating," he said, "what the earthquake is doing at the underside of the foundation."

The shake table was bolted to six large wheel assemblies that rolled back and forth on rails bolted to the concrete floor. A large actuator beneath the table, essentially a giant piston, pushed the structure back and forth. In mimicking the giant Tohoku quake of 2011, it would push the giant table and the plywood classroom on top of it up to a force of 1g, shaking it sideways with the same force that gravity exerts downwards.

The shaking started rocking back and forth steadily, but after about ten seconds the whole structure seemed to snap. It jolted back abruptly in the opposition direction, triggering a loud crack from the wood. When two kids jump in unison on a trampoline but fall slightly out of rhythm with each other, the trampoline will snap back on the person who falls a fraction of a second behind the other, starting its upward trajectory just before they finish their downward fall. As a result, the person who falls behind either bounces up or collapses on buckled knees. As the shake table continued rocking back and forth, the engineers watched for signs the horizontal pressure might make the wooden walls buckle. But when the shaking stopped two minutes later, the building was still standing.

The teams of engineers started inspecting the walls. They examined the plywood on the outside, but Taylor also wanted them to pay close attention to the drywall on the inside. "From my perspective the drywall is the canary," he explained, "because it shows the smallest cracks." Sure enough, small cracks were evident on the drywall and around the edges of some of the plywood as well. A few nails had also started to slip out a fraction of an inch. Overall, though, the room withstood considerable shaking reasonably well. The engineers finished their inspections and compared notes, and then the structure was tested and inspected again. Finally, on the third test, the pressure was increased by 25 percent. Once again, the structure remained standing.

This wasn't the shake table's first dance; it has conducted many tests since 2003. So the fact that the building didn't fall over was not much of a surprise to the engineers. Many similar tests in the past have shown them that plywood walls with enough nails are strong enough and flexible enough to withstand the most powerful earthquakes. They have also demonstrated how similar structures with horizontal boards (which are typically six inches wide), instead of plywood (which is typically four feet wide), can come apart and collapse during powerful shaking, because the narrower boards don't have the same lateral strength as the plywood and often fall off the vertical wood studs when their nails pop out.

The young engineers learning about post-quake inspection didn't see a building collapse at UBC that day. But they were honing important skills that will be in great demand right after a major earthquake: inspecting the buildings that are still standing to determine whether or not people can safely go back inside. Graham Taylor believes cities prone to big earthquakes will need many more trained inspectors than they have now. He also believes those cities will benefit from installing networks of instruments that measure the ground-force acceleration. Shaking can vary greatly from place to place, so knowing its exact strength at a precise location and combining it with specific knowledge of how different types of construction respond to different levels of shaking will help the inspectors. If readings showed a modern house with plywood walls on bedrock was subject to shaking at roughly half the force of gravity, an inspector could confirm that with a quick visual inspection, the homeowners could return much sooner, and the inspectors could move on to other houses. Cities like Victoria and Vancouver, Taylor insists, will be able to recover much more quickly from a major earthquake through this combination of training and technology.

—

While post-earthquake recovery will be important, reducing the risk ahead of time is essential. The long list of risks in Seattle has been apparent for decades, but some are more difficult to ignore than others, like the Alaskan Way Viaduct—the elevated double-deck section of state highway that funnelled a hundred thousand cars a day through downtown Seattle. The viaduct opened in 1953 and for decades served as a crucial transportation link. On one side were snow-capped mountains and the glistening waters of Elliott Bay; on the other, the city's sleek skyscrapers. As the years went on, however, the viaduct became a decrepit eyesore standing between the city and the ocean and mountain views. But no one seriously pushed to get rid of it until Washington State conducted a seismic assessment. Its conclusion was clear: despite being built with ten thousand tonnes of steel to reinforce the twenty-four thousand cubic yards of concrete, the viaduct was not designed to withstand a major earthquake, and its foundations were built on landfill, which was held in place by a seawall. In short, in an earthquake, the ground under the elevated freeway could liquefy. Some lengths of the roadway would pancake straight down while others would fall sideways and become engulfed in flames from the spontaneous gas explosions on the nearby wharves.

In 1989, when the Loma Prieta quake rocked the San Francisco Bay Area, Seattle residents watched the partial collapse of the strikingly similar Cypress Street Viaduct in Oakland and worried. Then the 2001 Nisqually earthquake cracked some of the Seattle viaduct's concrete columns and weakened some of its joints, and it was closed for repairs. Not long after it reopened to traffic, engineers said there was a one in twenty chance the highway would collapse in the next ten years. They recommended replacing it, but the heavy viaduct remained for years, settling into the soft ground in slow motion. In 2006 a group of scientists from the University of Washington urged the city to close the structure. But the traffic kept crawling, and so did the debate about what to do. Some groups wanted to replace the old viaduct with a new one designed to modern seismic codes, something that would also require significant repairs to the seawall. Finally, in 2009, the city, state, county, and port all agreed to replace the Alaskan Way Viaduct with a bored underground tunnel.

The Japanese company Hitachi Zosen built the world's largest tunnel-boring machine to burrow under the city. The TBM was shipped to Seattle in forty-one separate pieces. Fully assembled, the machine was ninety-nine metres long and weighed more than six thousand metric tonnes. The round cutter head, which would bore into the ground, was an astounding seventeen metres in diameter. Transportation planners named the colossal machine Bertha, after Bertha Knight Landes, the first woman to serve as mayor of Seattle or any major American city.

The tunnel itself was tall enough to fit a five-storey building and was bored more than two kilometres beneath the surface. It stretched under 158 different buildings, including many skyscrapers. Many of the buildings above were enormous, and yet allowing the ground under them to settle even a few inches could be enough to destabilize them dangerously. Adding to the challenge was the inconsistency of the ground. Engineers drilled six hundred test holes and discovered that it contained manmade fill, silt, sand, clay, rocks of many sizes, and a fair amount of water. Bertha was well-equipped to deal with all of these, but it would be slow going. The machine used more than seven hundred cutting tools on its face to dig out the giant tunnel, two metres at a time. Every time it moved on to the next two-metre stretch, workers needed to build another short circular portion of tunnel wall. They also drilled diagonal protective walls into the ground between the tunnel and the buildings above, pushing pipes into the earth and then filling them with concrete or grout.

Bertha the TBM started boring in 2013. Two state senators tried to kill the project before it was finished. But in 2017 Bertha emerged into the light of delay, more than two years late and, at $3 billion, considerably over budget. The steel components at the front of the massive drill were heavily damaged and had to be cut into manageable sections before they could be melted down and recycled. It would take a few more months to dismantle the rest of Bertha and move on to the work of building a two-level freeway and the necessary infrastructure inside the tunnel. The "race against the next earthquake," as Governor Jay Inslee called the viaduct replacement project, stretched years past its initial completion date, but the new tunnel finally opened to traffic early in 2019, and by the end of the year, the viaduct was gone, brought down by humans instead of nature.

"Earthquake!"

The word was barely out of Rob Dery's mouth before more than twenty grade four students scrambled under their desks. This was not a natural disaster, but a drill that had become an important part of kids' education at St. Patrick's Elementary, an independent Catholic school in Victoria. Euan Skinner, a parent who was involved in the school's earthquake preparations, stood watching at the side of the class. "You can see they're very quick," he said, breaking the brief silence that followed the drill. "Thank you, class!" The hum of chattering children resumed as the students clambered out from under their desks.

At first glance, the desks are unremarkable. Designed for two students sitting next to each other, the double desks are roughly the size of a refrigerator lying on its side. Each desk is essentially a rectangular steel box with a heavy tabletop that's supported by equally sturdy vertical steel plates that wrap around the whole desk. Under the desk are two square openings for the students with steel grab bars welded onto the sides for something to hold in the event of an earthquake. A triangular steel compartment acts as both a storage space for water, food, and emergency supplies and as a diagonal slope for the students to lean against while they hang onto the grab bars. These are LifeGuard desks, and they're built in Seattle. They're exceptionally strong. As Skinner points out, they're strong enough to support the weight of a collapsed building on top of them until rescuers can crawl inside or the students can crawl out.

That's what these desks are designed to do: remain standing even when the building they're in does not. A promotional video produced for LifeGuard Structures shows a series of destructive tests that demonstrate the desk's strength. In one test, a big yellow excavator dropped a giant concrete block onto a regular school desk and squashed it flat. When the same block was dropped onto a LifeGuard desk, it bounced off the top. Not satisfied with that demonstration, the testers then stacked up four blocks on one side of a desk and four more on the other side. The excavator lifted a giant concrete platform on top and placed another eight concrete blocks, weighing nearly three thousand pounds, on the platform. Once the whole pile was in place, the excavator knocked it over. The giant blocks tumbled down but bounced off the desk, which remained standing with little more than a few dents. They put both an old Jaguar sedan and a desk inside a car crusher. The Jag was well and truly flattened, but the desk still stood in its original shape. They also put a desk next to a concrete wall in an elementary school that was being demolished. The wall was knocked down onto the desk, and then a 102,000-pound excavator rumbled back and forth over the debris and the desk. When the piles of concrete and bent rebar were cleared away, the desk remained completely intact. (A man also fired on a desk with a .45-calibre handgun, without success, suggesting the desks might be marketed as a safeguard against school shootings.)

The video's most impressive seismic simulation, however, involved the demolition of the Oak Knoll Naval Hospital in Oakland, California. LifeGuard Structures put four desks inside the eleven-floor concrete tower, each painted a bright spring-green for easy identification after the collapse. One sat on the ground floor, another on the top floor, and two more on floors in between. A demolition team from Oklahoma used eight hundred pounds of explosives to bring the building down with the efficiency of many deadly earthquakes. Sixteen seconds was all it took from start to finish. Once the dust had cleared, and the excavators had picked their way through the rubble, all four desks were found, and all four desks were still intact. They were scraped and dented, but their structures were not compromised. It's possible that, in a freefall, one of these desks might tip and allow a piece of steel or concrete to strike the person inside. Still, the desks seem like a relatively simple way to give people a decent chance at surviving the total collapse of a concrete tower.

St. Patrick's Elementary is only three storeys high, but engineers concluded that most of the school, which was built in the 1950s, was prone to collapse. The good news was that it could be strengthened. The bad news was that it would be an expensive job and could take several years to complete. Nervous parents pondered what might happen to their kids if an earthquake struck before then, and together with school staff they decided the school would join an earthquake early-warning system with other Catholic schools in Victoria and Vancouver. The system was equipped with a unique warning siren, which sounds a lot like old air-raid warning sirens.

Systems like this are becoming more popular in the world's seismic zones. Japan and Mexico have embraced them as a practical means of giving millions of people a few brief but crucial moments to prepare before the shaking starts. Earthquake early warning can tell us when an earthquake has started and is on its way (it should not be confused with earthquake prediction, which will be discussed in a later chapter). That could give people in cities like Seattle and Vancouver a minute or more warning that one of the world's largest earthquakes is about to start shaking the ground beneath them. Where an earthquake ruptures closer to a city, the warning will be shorter. But even if it's only five seconds, it could be enough time to save lives.

Earthquake early-warning systems require some complicated engineering, but the basic principle behind how they work is simple. When a fault ruptures it sends out different types of waves. The P-wave speeds away from the epicentre first and provides seismic sensors with a warning that the slower-moving S-wave, which causes the shaking, is on its way. That warning can be shared almost immediately with any schools, utilities, and transportation providers that are connected to the seismic-monitoring network. The warning can also be shared directly with millions of people through emergency notifications on their cell phones. It's easy to underestimate the benefit of a short warning ahead of a disaster that will happen anyway. But for many people, a few seconds in a major quake could make all the difference. It could be enough time for a person to take cover under a desk or stop a high-speed train, for drivers to get off bridges and out of tunnels, for bridge and tunnel operators to close entry gates; enough time to send pre-programmed elevators to ground floors, and for utilities to shut down gas lines. In many respects, earthquake early-warning systems are a simple solution, but they require significant investments of time and money to build networks of sensors, design the alert systems, and monitor and maintain those systems once they're up and running. As with many other seismic safety measures, they require communities to make a choice to invest in their own safety.

The earthquake warning siren in St. Patrick's is loud and would likely give most staff and students enough time to jump under their desks. But what good would that be if the whole building collapsed seconds later? That's where the LifeGuard desks came in: the school bought the stronger, more expensive desks with the hope that they might keep its students alive, even if the building collapsed. "It's all a complete package," the school's principal, Deanne Paulson, says. "It makes the building as safe as we can make it with what we know is available."

Since St. Patrick's first bought those desks, the school has undergone a major seismic retrofit. The exterior concrete walls of the gymnasium and main building were strengthened, and the concrete foundations were reinforced. Steel bracing rods were connected to the wall columns, and steel attachments, called drag struts, were used to connect the walls to the floors and ceilings. These extra safety measures should keep the school standing, even in a major earthquake.

Making buildings safe sounds like a logical choice, but it often presents an emotional dilemma. For more than a century, thousands of people in Victoria have built a strong bond with Victoria High. This is the oldest public high school in Western Canada, originally housed in a two-room log cabin. The current version, the fourth Vic High, was built in 1914. Its ornate facade features tall columns and large arched windows over the entrances. Inside, it looks like a classic North American high school, and several movies have filmed in the four-storey building. The theatre has hosted countless political debates, high school plays, and graduation ceremonies. On a Saturday morning in April, hundreds of local residents gathered in one of the school's gymnasiums to discuss whether it should be torn down to make way for a new high school that won't crush a thousand students and staff during an earthquake.

The school district organized the open house to present three options to Victoria residents. The first was to spend between $50 million and $60 million to tear down the old building and replace it with a brand-new school. The district had already done that with two other schools: Oak Bay High and Sir James Douglas Elementary. The second option was to upgrade the old building, at a cost of $60 million to $70 million. The third option was to retain the historic facade of the building—for old time's sake, you might say—and build a new school behind that. That would cost $100 million to $110 million. One option that wasn't presented was to simply do nothing.

Most of those in attendance were seniors who had been students at the school decades ago. The school superintendent greeted people individually, answering a few questions but mostly listening to opinions. "There was a quake when I went here," a man in his sixties said authoritatively. "But it's still standing." The superintendent replied patiently, pointing out what scientists have discovered about giant quakes here in the half-decade since this former student felt a minor earthquake in his youth. Some people followed a pair of teenagers on a guided school tour. They shuffled through smelly change rooms, up wide stairwells, and into a locker-lined hallway. A seventy-something woman stopped suddenly and looked as though she'd seen a ghost. "I was standing right here when they said John Kennedy was shot," she recalled.

The group continued around a corner and walked between walls hung with pictures of past graduating classes. The young guides tried to lead them to the end of the hallway, but the smiling faces from bygone days proved too much to pass by. Some stopped at the black-and-white portraits from the 1930s, while a silver-haired man silently studied the 1945 graduating class photo. Most examined the photographs from the 1950s, when the class sizes started to swell. The student population peaked in the late sixties, as sideburns and long hair started to dominate the sepia-toned pictures.

"There used to be fifteen hundred students in this school," one of the teenage guides noted. "But we only have eight hundred and fifty now."

Back in the gym, the attendees were invited to take markers and write their thoughts on Post-it Notes to put up on the wall: "Victoria is losing its charm and character one building at a time," one note read. "Please save this one!" Another pleaded: "Don't tear down a castle." And a third: "We're losing a Victoria landmark!" Most of the people who came to the open house had a similar message for the school district. While many agreed Vic High should be made safer, only a few said they wanted a new building.

School trustees had a difficult decision: rebuilding looked like the cheapest option, and one that would provide extra space for students and community groups in the future. But tearing down the oldest high school in Western Canada would be incredibly unpopular. One thing was clear, though: the school district needed to act. Seismic engineers had evaluated Vic High more than once and were unequivocal: it would all come crashing down in a major quake. A strengthened school would not only remain standing but could also be used as a makeshift shelter, impromptu medical clinic, or emergency command centre after a disaster. It could save lives *and* play an indispensable role in recovery.

While community members scribbled their thoughts on Post-it Notes, a larger message loomed above them on the gymnasium wall, the words painted in both Latin and English. *Palma non sine pulvere*: there is no reward without effort. Elected officials seemed to take the message to heart. In an effort at compromise, the school district voted to preserve the school's heritage and opt for a more expensive seismic upgrade. The effort would require more than the sizable price tag: the school would have to be closed for two years for construction and its students bussed to an empty school a few kilometres away. But the reward may be lives saved and a community strengthened.

Unsafe schools are not the only problem. Up the east coast of Vancouver Island, the city of Campbell River is downstream from two earth-filled dams, just two of the many hydroelectric dams built in British Columbia and the Pacific Northwest that provide power to millions of people—and that could fail in a major quake. The John Hart and Strathcona Dams are owned by BC Hydro, a publicly owned utility. Both were built in the 1940s and 1950s. Like many structures of that era, they were not designed to withstand a major earthquake with shaking that lasts three minutes or more.

In the last decade, BC Hydro has spent millions to assess its dams, and the results are sobering. If the John Hart Dam fails, BC Hydro estimates a wall of water as high as eleven metres could swamp Campbell River, home to thirty-five thousand people, in less than an hour. If the Strathcona Dam fails, it would take closer to two and half hours for the surge of water to reach Campbell River, but the effects would still be catastrophic. BC Hydro has identified a number of measures that could reduce the risk significantly, but they will take decades to complete and cost billions.

First, BC Hydro tackled the John Hart Dam's generating station. Water flowed from the reservoir downhill to the generating station through a series of massive tunnels, some made of wood, to reach the six giant turbines that generate electricity. Both the generating station and the tunnels were likely to collapse in an earthquake. They could have been strengthened, but BC Hydro concluded that would be prohibitively expensive, so engineers decided to replace both with a tunnel so massive that it could fill an Olympic swimming pool every twenty seconds. That water would rush into a giant underground cavern, ten storeys tall, that houses three new hydroelectric turbines. Those turbines would create a little more electricity than the six old ones—enough for about eighty thousand homes. But the main improvement for the people who live downstream would be the new, much deeper, outlet, which could allow dam managers to drain the giant reservoir much more quickly after a quake.

But more improvements to the John Hart Dam are required, such as the strengthening of upstream berms. Crucially, the five-hundred-metre-wide Strathcona Dam needs to have new emergency spillway outlets added to its lower half. If the giant earth-filled dam were seriously damaged in a quake today, engineers could release only a small proportion of the water stored behind it by using flood protection methods.

Other dams may fare better in massive earthquakes. The US Army Corps of Engineers manages many of the big dams in Washington and Oregon. They perform a general safety inspection on each dam every five years and a seismic study every fifteen years to assess the risk of a dam failure following a magnitude-9 Cascadia Subduction Zone quake. While many dams were built before the earthquake risk was known, engineers say large structures, like the 141-metre-high Detroit Dam in northwest Oregon, were designed with massive concrete slabs attached together with joints. These joints give the dam flexibility in changing temperatures, and as a result engineers believe concrete dams will hold, even in a major earthquake.

They strike a more cautious note when discussing earth-filled dams. The Cougar Dam, eighty kilometres east of the city of Eugene, is a rock-fill hydroelectric dam that's almost five hundred metres long. If the dam were to fail, it could threaten the safety of approximately 160,000 people who live in Eugene, and that isn't the only dam in the region. The US Army Corps of Engineers is reluctant to share its flood prediction maps, but it has let some local residents look at them, and the *Register-Guard* reported that one envisions the McKenzie River reaching the fourth floor of the Sacred Heart Medical Center in Springfield, near Eugene.

For now, the dams remain vulnerable. Because BC Hydro may not finish full seismic remediation of the Campbell River dams until sometime in the 2030s, local officials are putting their efforts into training residents in what to do if an earthquake strikes. In 2014 the protective services coordinator with the Strathcona Regional District, Shaun Koopman, started including residents in drills that saw them walk or cycle to pre-planned locations on high ground, sixty seconds after the imaginary shaking stopped and before a massive torrent of water could reach them. "We did the drills with our first responders," he said, "but we needed the public to practise, too."

But in other coastal communities the real fear is what will happen when the water rushes up. The Pacific Ocean presents a deadly threat to low-lying coastal towns in Cascadia: when the sea floor shakes hard enough, it will trigger a tsunami. And if past is prologue, the Japanese tsunami of 2011 offers an ominous warning of seismic tempests to come.

Chapter 3
THE PACIFIC'S DEADLY ECHO

On a cool March afternoon in Japan's Tohoku region, in the port city of Otsuchi, Marley Daviduk and Carisa Webster stood a few steps away from the water. The animal-rights activists had flown more than seven thousand kilometres from Vancouver Island to make a documentary film for the Sea Shepherd Conservation Society about Japan's contentious Dall's porpoise hunt. They'd just shot video footage of hunting ships returning to port and were standing with five other volunteers when the seawall started swaying beneath their feet.

Tremors are a common occurrence in Japan, and for many Japanese people the first few seconds of this one didn't seem all that different from countless others. But the shaking got stronger as it continued, and before long it became apparent this was no ordinary earthquake. After a minute of rumbling, the ocean floor east of the island of Honshu showed no signs of stopping. It carried on right through the two-minute mark, then three, four, and five minutes. By the time the earth stopped moving, this monster magnitude-9 earthquake had lasted roughly six minutes.

Though stunned, Daviduk and Webster were not hurt. Their colleague Scott West urged them to jump into the car they'd driven to the port. A tsunami was coming, he predicted, and they needed to get to high ground. The group knew exactly where to go. Searching for a good place to shoot footage, they had recently discovered a roadside viewpoint high on a hill overlooking the town. It took them only a few minutes to make their way uphill, but when they arrived and looked back down they saw a horrific scene in the city below.

Tsunami warning signs invariably depict a giant cresting wave, but what Daviduk, Webster, and West actually saw was the ocean rising quickly and flooding much of Otsuchi. The water then flowed back out, pulling boats, cars, and whole houses along with it. It exposed the ocean floor as it receded and then, a few minutes later, an even bigger wave rushed in, causing more destruction. Wave after giant wave pounded the crippled city for several hours. Otsuchi had a tsunami wall, but the waves were at least double its size, Daviduk said, and the water "ripped it to pieces and tossed it around like it was made of Styrofoam." Her experience has convinced Daviduk that cities and towns shouldn't be located in tsunami inundation zones, "because if you're at water level when that hits, if you don't get out, there is no surviving it."

Otsuchi was not the tsunami's only victim, but it was hit especially hard. Half an hour after the quake, a rush of frigid water crashed through the doors and windows of the city hall, just as municipal officials were discussing how to respond to the disaster. Of the one hundred people inside the building, only ten managed to escape to the roof. The tsunami killed more than eight hundred people in Otsuchi; five years later, more than half of them were still listed as missing. Ten percent of the town's pre-disaster population had simply disappeared.

Across Japan, nineteen thousand people were killed, with more than two thousand others missing and presumed drowned. Six thousand more were injured and roughly four hundred thousand buildings suffered either total or partial collapse, including structures three kilometres inland. In all, more than three hundred thousand people were forced to find temporary homes.

The waves destroyed most of the fishing industry in Iwate and Miyagi prefectures; boats, processing plants, and whole ports were either flattened or washed out to sea. Significant stretches of railroad were also wiped out. The Fukushima Daiichi nuclear power plant shut down during the earthquake but lost its emergency cooling system when the tsunami overtopped the plant, which caused the meltdown of three nuclear reactors. More than 150,000 people in the twenty-kilometre radius of the plant had to evacuate their homes. Five years after the disaster, nearly a hundred thousand still hadn't returned. Radiation permeated rice paddies, vegetable fields, and cattle stocks, costing many farmers their livelihoods. The disaster also sent five million tonnes of debris floating across the Pacific Ocean. Most of it sank, but more than a million tonnes drifted on the surface. Significant deposits washed up on North American beaches years later.

Hours later, when the waves finally subsided, the landscape in Otsuchi looked like a bomb had gone off. Fires dotted the horizon, boats hung suspended in trees, and the corpses of people and animals lay scattered among the wreckage.

The epicentre of the quake was 130 kilometres off the coast of Japan and stretched over an area some five hundred kilometres long by two hundred kilometres wide. When the Pacific plate slid under the continental plate along the Japan Trench, a patch of the ocean's floor roughly the size of South Korea rose up and sent the tsunami waves crashing into the Japanese coastline. The height of the waves depended on the topography of the coastline wherever the wave came ashore. In some instances, the tsunami measured between three and seven metres. In other instances, where the waves met a steep hill or mountain, the water rose up to forty metres above sea level.

The earthquake originated in the same type of offshore megathrust subduction zone as the Cascadia Subduction Zone, and the devastation unleashed on Japan offers an ominous warning to

Cascadia. Although the Tohoku quake was the largest ever recorded in Japan, it was not without precedent. In 2011, even before the shaking stopped, earthquake researcher Masanobu Shishikura of Japan's National Institute of Advanced Science and Technology worried about what was coming next, because of what happened along the same subduction zone more than eleven centuries earlier. Paleo-seismologists, who study historic earthquakes, estimate that the 869 Sanriku earthquake was a magnitude 8.4 (it may have been higher) and that it triggered a devastating tsunami that flooded the Sendai plain, which is also located in the Tohoku region. "I knew that the people would not be saved unless they immediately started running," Shishikura said. "I just kept praying, wondering if people there were evacuating properly."

The size of the waves simply wasn't predicted and took many Japanese emergency officials by surprise. The same miscalculations that led to the construction of tsunami walls that were too low also led many homeowners to the mistaken belief that their homes were high enough to be safe. As a result of those inaccurate pre-disaster assurances, they didn't seek higher ground when they should have. The waves swept them off the tops of buildings they believed were tall enough to keep them safe, carrying them to their deaths.

At Okawa elementary school in the village of Kamaya, the tsunami killed seventy-four of the seventy-eight students and ten of the eleven teachers. The school was at the foot of a forested hill that rose more than two hundred metres above sea level, and even the youngest students could have climbed out of harm's way long before the tsunami struck. But the school stood four kilometres from the ocean, and school and civic officials underestimated the risk. They delayed evacuation for more than forty-five minutes after the earthquake. They even convinced several parents who came to retrieve their children that it would be safer to leave them at school. Finally, as tsunami warnings came in, teachers argued about where to go. They decided to walk to higher ground near a bridge, but it was too late. The water surged over the banks of the Kitakami River, and the children could not escape.

For parents, the knowledge that their children could have simply walked to safety compounded the tragedy. Some suffered a further anguish: their children's bodies could not be found. The post-tsunami devastation was so widespread that firefighters resorted to excavators to find bodies, but the official search was eventually called off before all of the bodies were found. Naomi Hiratsuka was not willing to abandon the search for her twelve-year-old daughter, Koharu, so she obtained an excavator's license and continued the search herself. Five months after the tsunami, a body was found floating near the mouth of the river, and DNA tests confirmed it was Koharu. "Finding her made a big difference to my husband and me," the grieving mother said. "We could have a funeral and cremate her. She had come home to us."

Two years after the tsunami, parents sued the local government for failing to protect their children. The court awarded them several million dollars, a hollow victory if ever there was one.

Since the start of modern earthquake measurement in the nineteenth century, only three quakes have exceeded the 2011 Japanese disaster in magnitude, and only one of those had a higher death toll. The Indian Ocean earthquake and tsunami struck on December 26, 2004, off the coast of the Indonesian island of Sumatra. The US Geological Survey calculated the magnitude at 9.1. The rupture of the fault lasted three to four minutes, but the shaking was felt for as long as ten minutes on some parts of northern Sumatra.

The geological event was breathtaking, and the humanitarian catastrophe that followed was heartbreaking. More than two hundred thousand people were killed in fourteen different countries, though the exact number may be considerably higher. Indonesia was closest to the rupture zone and suffered the most. Estimates vary from 130,000 deaths all the way up to 220,000 in Indonesia alone. Tens of thousands more died in Sri Lanka, India, and Thailand. The killer waves even claimed lives in South Africa, a full eight thousand kilometres away. For many of those who survived, life was a misery. More than 1.7 million people around the Indian Ocean were displaced.

While the earthquake had a devastating impact, it was the tsunami that claimed the most lives overall. The waves swelled up to thirty metres above sea level along some parts of the coast of Sumatra. The sudden upward motion of the seabed displaced a stunning amount of ocean water, resulting in huge tsunami waves that travelled east and west. In deep water, the tsunami caused what looked like a small wave on the surface. That small wave spread quickly in all directions at anywhere from five hundred to one thousand kilometres an hour, roughly the speed of a jetliner. But as the waves approached coastlines and moved into shallower water, they slowed and swelled into deadly forces of nature that wiped whole towns off the map.

The absence of a tsunami warning system, a key safety component, compounded the tragedy. While Japan and North America benefit from a network of buoys and undersea sensors, the populous nations of the Indian Ocean had no such safeguard in 2004. No doubt many thousands of lives would have been saved if tsunami warning sirens had existed to prompt people to run for high ground before the waves reached the shore. Tragically, many victims also would have survived if they had simply known more about tsunamis, as the remarkable story of a ten-year-old girl from England illustrates.

Tilly Smith and her family were on holiday in Phuket, Thailand, on the day of the tsunami. Standing on the beach not long before the disaster, she saw warning signs similar to those she'd recently studied in school. "The sea was all frothy like on the top of a beer," she recalled. "It was bubbling." Convinced that a deadly wave was on the way, she tried to persuade her mother to run up to the hotel. Her mother hesitated, and Tilly resorted to screaming. Everyone on the beach followed her up to safety, and Tilly Smith was later credited with saving one hundred lives.

That you should run for high ground immediately after an earthquake was new information to Tilly Smith but very old to ancient tribes. Ten days after the tsunami smashed ashore, members of the Jarawa tribe, on the Andaman Islands in the Indian Ocean, emerged from the forest to confirm that all 250 people in their community had survived. Tribe members were suspicious of outsiders and did not reveal much about their ordeal, but a few of them spoke limited Hindi and told Indian government officials that their oral history warned that a huge wall of water might follow the shaking of the earth. As a result, tribespeople who had been fishing along the shore when the ground shook ran up into the forest immediately.

In contrast the Nicobarese people, who are thought to have moved to the islands only five hundred years ago, suffered greatly. The official death toll in the Andaman and Nicobar islands was roughly 1,300 people with more than 5,000 missing. Would they have known to run to high ground if their ancestors lived through previous tsunamis? Perhaps. Or perhaps it is more a case of being in the wrong place at the wrong time. The Indigenous tribes that fared well typically spent more time on higher ground, away from the coast, than the unlucky Nicobarese. While there are certainly other factors involved, people who know they need to seek high ground have a better chance of survival than those who do not. That knowledge will likely save lives in British Columbia and the US Pacific Northwest when the Cascadia Subduction Zone ruptures. If the full five hundred kilometres of the fault rips, a long section of crust that's been pulled down will snap back up suddenly, thrusting a huge wall of water towards the coast at a terrifying speed. The first waves could hit dry land in less than fifteen minutes. Heights will vary depending on location, but in coastal communities that face the open ocean it will be terrifying. Anyone in the tsunami inundation zone will need to get to high ground quickly, and they'll have to stay there for many hours. As was the case in Japan and the Indian Ocean, the Cascadia tsunami will send multiple waves, some of which may be higher than the first, for hours after the earthquake.

On Vancouver Island, tsunami waves and currents could reach as high as fifteen metres along some stretches of the coast, posing a huge threat to communities like Port Alberni, Tofino, and Ucluelet. Some communities in Washington State are even more vulnerable. The town of Westport sits at the end of a peninsula at the mouth of Grays Harbor. Ninety-nine percent of the developed land and 89 percent of the town's people are located in the tsunami zone. The town of two thousand is often filled with thousands of tourists, but many of them will be too far from high ground to get to safety before a tsunami crashes ashore. To make matters worse, much of the town is built on sand and is expected to liquefy during the quake. A little farther south, many people on the Long Beach Peninsula are even farther away from high ground. Long Beach is described as the longest beach in the lower forty-eight states, stretching forty-five kilometres north to south. It's a long drive from the tip of the peninsula to high ground, even if the ground doesn't liquefy and power lines don't fall on roads.

Other towns are closer to high ground but face similar challenges. In Seaside, Oregon, the population of six thousand can swell to forty thousand at the height of tourist season. Most of the town is no higher than five metres above sea level, which is well below the maximum projected tsunami heights of more than twenty metres, and it could be difficult to get to the hills that surround the town because Seaside's bridges are vulnerable to collapse, and much of the town is built on sand that is expected to liquefy.

There are two other distinct threats to Oregon, Washington, and British Columbia: localized tsunamis that are created by undersea landslides and can strike within minutes, and distant tsunamis that are generated from faraway earthquakes.

The Great Alaska Earthquake caused both of these. On Good Friday, March 27, 1964, it shook the state with astonishing force and didn't stop for four minutes and thirty-eight seconds. At magnitude 9.2, the quake was the second largest ever recorded and the largest ever recorded in North America. It rumbled to life fifteen miles under the waters of Prince William Sound, where the Pacific plate subducts below the North American plate. The five-hundred-mile-long rupture released roughly the same energy as two thousand magnitude-7 earthquakes. While the shaking on the ground was intense and caused twelve deaths, the earthquake's effect on the ocean was even more frightening.

The surging waters reached as high as seventy metres in Valdez Arm. Though lower in the Port of Valdez, they were still deadly. When the shaking started, many of the town's residents were at the dock to greet the first ship to dock at Valdez that spring, SS *Chena*. The ship's arrival was a big occasion because it brought money, supplies, and fresh fruit. The crew was renowned for throwing candy to anyone standing on the dock. But what should have been a special day turned horrific in an instant. The harbour and docks collapsed soon after the shaking started, dragging down adults and children alike. Frantic crew on board the *Chena* tried to rescue them but did not have enough time. The liquefaction of the sand and gravel underneath Valdez caused a large section of the delta to slide into the water and produced a local tsunami, roughly nine metres high, that smashed ashore before the shaking had even stopped. To make matters worse, tanks at the Union Oil Company ruptured, sparking a fire that finished off the few buildings still standing. In total, thirty-two people died in Valdez.

The vertical movement of the ocean floor generated its own tectonic tsunami that sped across the ocean on a deadly path. Authorities on Kodiak Island had time to warn many people to head for higher ground. But the notice had the opposite effect on fishermen, who instead ran down to the docks to try to rescue their boats. Six fishermen and nine other residents were killed, and Kodiak's oil, crab, and fishing facilities were wiped out.

Meanwhile, another deadly tsunami sped southwards. When it reached Vancouver Island, the first wave was funnelled up the Alberni Inlet and into Port Alberni in the middle of the night. The first wave was smaller than the second, and it acted as a warning to people in the town, who moved to higher ground and escaped the full devastation of the six-metre wave that followed. The wave flattened much of the city's business district, but no one died in Port Alberni.

Farther down the Oregon coast, near Newport, Rita and Monte McKenzie and their four young children were sleeping in a tent at Beverly Beach State Park when the first wave hit. The tent filled, and the children screamed and scrambled to get their heads above water. Monte later told his pastor that logs lying on the beach "were thrown at us like matchsticks." When the second wave hit, all four kids and the family dog were swept out to sea. "I had two of the kids by the hands, but I have no idea what happened," Rita McKenzie told a reporter. "Nobody had a chance." All four of the McKenzies' children, ages three to eight, died; only six-year-old Ricky's body was found.

The tsunamis continued south to California. The biggest waves to hit Crescent City were actually bigger than much of what had struck Oregon, because the offshore geography, or bathymetry as it's known to scientists, makes this stretch of California's coast particularly susceptible to tsunamis. Officials in Crescent City had been warned and had passed on the warnings to the three thousand residents. But people had grown accustomed to hearing the warnings with little or no wave coming ashore, and by 1964 many simply ignored them.

The tsunami ravaged twenty-nine city blocks. Eight adults and two children died, and one hundred people were left homeless. Buildings were swept off their foundations, cars scattered like toys, and food spoiled inside flooded supermarkets. Two days later, on Easter Sunday, shocked residents filled the local churches. "This points out the transiency of all things material," Reverend RW Huber told parishioners at Grace Lutheran Church. "We can be well-to-do one moment and poverty stricken the next."

Other West Coast tsunamis are more difficult to predict than those that come from subduction zone earthquakes. One frightening possibility in British Columbia is in the Fraser River delta. The Fraser discharges about seventeen million tonnes of sediment every year, and the western front of the delta is susceptible to underwater landslides. Those could be triggered by an earthquake, or the unconsolidated sediment could simply collapse under its own weight with no seismic trigger. Either way, the tsunami could be big and fast. Scientists estimate a tsunami of eighteen metres could sweep across the Georgia Strait and strike Galiano Island. In the Vancouver suburb of Richmond, where dikes separate much of the low-lying land from the ocean, talk of any tsunami makes emergency officials nervous. But scientists have suggested the delta foreshore would deflect and reduce wave energy, which means that any tsunami hitting the heavily populated Vancouver suburbs would not be higher than two metres.

At least three river deltas in Washington State also pose a tsunami risk. The Puyallup, Snohomish, and Duwamish Rivers empty into Puget Sound. The Duwamish River is an industrialized waterway that runs twenty kilometres from Green River to Elliott Bay, in the shadows of downtown Seattle's skyscrapers and directly above the Seattle fault. If any of these three river deltas slump, they could generate a large local tsunami in a heavily populated area. But delta slope failures aren't the only risk in and around Seattle.

When the Seattle Fault Zone ruptures, or the Tacoma or South Whidbey Island faults, the floor of Puget Sound could either drop suddenly or be thrust upwards in a jolt that could generate a deadly tsunami. Scientists believe the ocean floor south of the Seattle fault rose between five and seven metres in the fault's last major rupture, roughly 1,100 years ago. They estimate a six-kilometre-long band of ocean floor lifted up a huge volume of water that surged north onto Whidbey Island. If that were to happen today, the damage would be staggering.

But Seattle is a city famous for technology and innovation, so it's no surprise that some of the people who live there are trying to engineer safety responses to the seismic risk. Forty kilometres north of downtown Seattle, in the pretty waterfront town of Mukilteo, an aerospace engineer has spent years working on an unusual tool. Julian Sharpe grew up in England but eventually settled here, close to Paine Field, where Boeing started building 747s in the 1960s, and embarked on a career in aviation. His particular specialty was aviation stress engineering, working for various companies to make sure their planes were safe to fly. But on a family vacation on the Oregon coast, lying in bed in an inn just a block or two from the beach, listening to the waves, he started wondering what he could do if a tsunami hit. "And I thought, well, I could probably design and build something to jump into rather than having to haul everybody up the hill."

Sharpe started imagining a spherical escape pod that would keep the water out while keeping the people inside safe. To get a better sense of what the pod would need to withstand, he consulted with Eddie Bernard, an oceanographer who has studied tsunamis since the 1970s and led many studies at the National Oceanic and Atmospheric Administration. Sharpe designed a structure that was not just waterproof but also flame-resistant, lightweight, and incredibly strong.

"What the tsunami and churning water does to the human body is horrific," Sharpe says bluntly. People who somehow survive the tsunami itself still face the risk of being impaled on sharp objects, burned in fires, or drowned. Sharpe designed an escape pod that is now sold as the Survival Capsule. It is made of aircraft-grade aluminum and lined on the interior walls with a thermal insulation blanket that's about a quarter of an inch thick and is similar to the re-entry tile used on space shuttles. The inside is basic but includes seats and harness seat belts similar to what is found in a race car, small bullet-proof glass portholes, and a locking marine door that keeps the water out, even under high pressure. It also has vents that can be opened to let air in and water bladders below the seats to provide buoyancy and stop the capsule from spinning out of control like a soccer ball. Those bladders also provide drinking water, just in case the occupants are stranded for a long time.

Sharpe designed several different sizes of escape pod ranging from a two-person model up to a sphere big enough for sixteen. He has had hundreds of orders from dozens of countries around the world, mostly Japan (he hopes to convince Japanese school officials to put the biggest pods on school roofs as a last resort for students and staff); only a few of his customers are in North America.

Jeanne Johnson was Sharpe's first American customer. She made the decision after moving from Seattle to Long Beach Peninsula, where she lives in a modern two-storey home near the beach. Oceanographers predict that a magnitude-9 full rip of the subduction zone will create a giant tsunami that will wash over the whole length of the peninsula, about fifteen minutes after the earthquake. Most or all of the sandy ground could liquefy, and none of the land on the peninsula is high enough to offer refuge from the surging water. The only way out, it seems, will be the long thin road that connects the end of the peninsula with the mainland. Johnson imagined thousands of panicking people trying to get down that road and started to think about an aquatic escape instead. For about $13,500, she purchased a two-person Survival Capsule, which she keeps in her garage. "If we get a nine-point-zero earthquake I've got to be able to get to it," Johnson says. "And we could have liquefaction beneath it, so it's on a concrete pad."

Inside the airtight marine door, a small sanctuary is packed full of emergency supplies: life jackets and helmets, enough dry food to sustain two people for forty days, extra clothes, nylon blankets, a first-aid kit, canisters with ten hours' worth of oxygen, an emergency radio transmitter, and more. Johnson can name every item by memory. She is quick to point out that she's not "one of those end-of-the-world preppers." She is, however, realistic about where she lives and the risks she faces. This comes from personal experience: as a young mother in Oklahoma, she had close calls with two tornadoes, and she was living in New Orleans when Hurricane Katrina hit. While she concedes she can't say for sure that the capsule will help her survive a tsunami, she thinks her preparations have increased her chances significantly.

Emergency planners have asked locals why they don't just move away. But a walk over the high dunes that stand between her house and the vast expanse of the Pacific Ocean, bald eagles soaring overhead, the slow sweeping sound of the waves crescendoing into a roar, makes it easy to see why this place would be hard to leave. And, Johnson says, "Where would we go? California has fires. Florida has hurricanes. The Midwest has tornadoes. You can't run from nature."

While some people hope to survive on their own, others are making preparations as a community. Farther up the Washington coast is the town of Westport, a busy fishing port that hauls in millions of pounds of crab, salmon, and hake every year, and thousands of tourists, too. But Westport has almost no natural defence against the sea. Sitting at the end of another vulnerable peninsula, it stands just above sea level, with small thickets of Sitka spruce, pine, and willow bent permanently by the same steady wind that makes it a popular destination for the windsurfing crowd. Almost no one in town at the time of a major earthquake would have enough time to escape a tsunami. So after years of discussion, the town decided to build a form of high ground.

Ocosta Elementary School stands on the main road out of town, about five kilometres from the centre of Westport. Seen from the road, nothing about the building marks it as unusual. But this is more than just a school: it is the first publicly funded vertical tsunami evacuation shelter in North America. The school's gymnasium is designed to withstand not only a major earthquake but also a major tsunami. The gymnasium's four corner towers are made of steel-reinforced concrete that extends deep beneath the surface. Each tower contains a wide staircase that's big enough to let a lot of people climb to the top quickly. Though the four towers are connected by the gym walls, those walls are engineered to give way and let most of the force of a tsunami wave flow through the structure at ground level. The four towers are designed to remain standing, and they support a grid of steel beams that form a large roof designed to hold the weight of two thousand people.

On the wall inside the school principal's office are two clearly marked emergency alarm switches protected under clear plastic. The one on the right is labeled LOCKDOWN: the principal can push it if the American plague of school shootings ever visits this small town. The alarm on the left looks like a standard fire-alarm lever found all over North America, but painted blue instead of red, and it's labelled TSUNAMI. If this lever is pulled, the sets of double doors at the bottom of each tower, which are normally locked, will unlock and open automatically.

"We can get the six hundred students on campus up here in about five and a half minutes," says school principal David Dooley, standing on the roof. "We can put the high school kids here, and the elementary kids over on the other side." The open ocean is a little more than a kilometre away. To the east lie the more protected waters of Grays Harbor. "If you look at the predictions, the ground here will drop. We may be the only place that's out of the water."

But the roof is exposed to the elements. The rain and wind would make it cold, and aftershocks would add to the ordeal for frightened children whose homes may have just been swept away. It's also possible that the roof may not be high enough to withstand the biggest tsunami that Cascadia could muster. Dooley nonetheless believes the structure will be the town's best bet after a major earthquake and that it will improve life in the meantime. "We found that kids feel safer here than any other place," he says. "It's nice that our community invested in the long-term safety of the people here."

The pretty tourist town of Seaside, Oregon, is mostly built on sand. Most of the downtown hotels stand on a spit of land between the pounding ocean waves and the final stretch of the Necanicum River, which runs parallel to the coast before it turns and empties into the surf. As a result, Seaside depends on its fourteen bridges, which support more than eighty thousand vehicle crossings each day. Some of the bridges are relatively modern; a few date back to the 1920s and '30s. Bridges are a lifeline out of the tsunami inundation zone and up into the hills, but not one is expected to remain usable after a major earthquake.

Doug Dougherty has been driving back and forth across those bridges for decades, wondering and worrying about what will happen in the Big One. As a long-time school superintendent, Dougherty has specific concerns about students and school staff. He's had each school evaluated: "Each one came back with a highly likely chance of catastrophic collapse in a Cascadia earthquake." And anyone who manages to get out of a collapsed building—an especially difficult task for those in classrooms without windows—will likely find collapsed bridges blocking their escape.

In the early 1990s, when he was principal of Cannon Beach

Elementary School, Dougherty found an old aerial photograph taken shortly after the 1964 Alaska tsunami tore down the Pacific coast. "It scoured the area," he recalled. "It took houses and bridges out, and I knew at that point that I needed to move the schools." At the time, scientists had only recently concluded the Cascadia Subduction Zone was capable of producing the world's largest earthquakes. They were still trying to calculate the size of the tsunamis it might produce. Dougherty, meanwhile, was promoted to superintendent, and despite being told by many people in his community that it wasn't his responsibility, he kept raising the issue of school safety and asking what would happen if a tsunami swept through.

The Oregon Department of Geology and Mineral Industries decided to investigate. What began as a modest two-week study eventually morphed into a multi-year investigation funded in part by the Federal Emergency Management Agency. Engineers drilled for geologic evidence of past quakes and tsunamis at several points along the Oregon coast. They found evidence that in the past, tsunami waves had reached heights of thirty metres.

The solution seemed obvious to Dougherty: simply move the schools uphill, to the outskirts of town. Dougherty and his team spent years negotiating a plan that would see all three schools closed and rebuilt on a new hillside campus that started forty-five metres uphill and rose to ninety metres above sea level at the top. Weyerhaeuser, a forest company, owned the land. In total, the plan to buy the land and build a new school campus had an estimated price tag of $128 million. But, as anyone who's ever sold insurance knows, convincing someone to spend money now against future risk can be a tough sell. The state of Oregon would not pay, citing a bizarre provision that any school in a tsunami inundation zone was ineligible for seismic retrofit funds. And a ban at the time on federal contributions to projects like this one let the federal government off the hook, too. That left the local taxpayers. In 2014 the city asked residents to vote on the plan and proposed a tax increase to fund the project that would amount to a few hundred dollars per year for the average homeowner. Residents rejected the measure by a nearly two-to-one margin.

But Dougherty didn't give up. He kept talking to local residents, especially the ones who just wanted him to stop. He also retired and volunteered all of his time as the project leader to keep costs down. His team continued its negotiations with Weyerhaeuser and convinced the company to donate eighty acres just east of town and above the tsunami inundation zone. By 2016 they'd cut costs to just under $100 million, thanks to the donated land and various small efficiencies to the school's design and configuration, and took their new pared-down plan back to Seaside voters. Enough of them changed their minds: they voted to move their children uphill and out of harm's way once and for all.

On a scorching hot July day, not long after I talked to Doug Dougherty, I turned onto a gravel logging road for the eighty-kilometre drive to the coastal village of Bamfield, the last leg of a Vancouver Island road trip. Becky, my wife, refereed our three sons in the back seat. We bumped along the rutted road for more than two hours, on a roughly parallel course with the Alberni Inlet that funnelled the Alaska tsunami waves in 1964. Just before we reached Bamfield we turned south and rolled into the Pachena Bay campground, which is operated by the Huu-ay-aht First Nation. At the side of the road, a large sign, 1700 TSUNAMI, stood as a historical reminder and future warning. On a site where Huu-ay-aht ancestors were swept to their deaths, we set up our tent and took a short stroll to the big sandy beach through ferns, salal bushes, and towering Douglas fir. We splashed in exposed tidal pools at low tide and walked the length of the beach, keeping an eye out for black bears.

The tide came up after dark, and I woke in the middle of the night to the measured, sweeping whooshes of big waves on the beach. I soon found myself thinking of the McKenzie family, swept out of their tent on an Oregon beach decades earlier. What was it like to go home to Tacoma without their children? Did they replay those frantic final moments in their minds, over and over again? How did they carry on with their lives after such a terrible loss?

I got out of the tent before the sun was up and strolled along the straight dirt road that runs the length of the Pachena Bay campground. Our tent was pitched at the far south end of the campground, right next to the start of the West Coast Trail. The trail is now primarily thought of as a test of physical endurance that takes hikers several days to traverse, but it was built more than a century ago so rescuers could reach survivors of shipwrecks along a stretch of coast so treacherous that sailors knew it as the Graveyard of the Pacific. The trail is a reminder that natural hazards are nothing new, and neither is the human desire to survive.

With tsunamis in mind, I had started the timer on my iPhone when I left the tent. It took me eight minutes to walk to the campground office. A tsunami-warning sign instructed campers to leave the campground, go through the village of Anacla, over the bridge towards Bamfield, and up the road that leads to Huu-ay-aht House, an impressive longhouse built up above the tsunami inundation zone. I guessed it would take us more than fifteen minutes to walk to high ground from our campsite if an earthquake struck, but I suspected we'd probably be running.

"Try not to worry about tsunamis," I've told my kids on the rare occasion when the topic comes up. "If you're anywhere near the ocean when there's an earthquake, just run uphill as fast as you can." But standing in the middle of a long, flat road in the forest, the ocean pounding the beach, my confidence wavered. If a tsunami was rushing towards us right now, I wondered, would we have enough time to escape?

Chapter 4
MOUNTAINS OF FIRE

Though the two men shared the same name, the Harry Truman who lived on Mount St. Helens in southern Washington State was not related to the thirty-third president of the United States. Harry Randall Truman had lived in isolation beside a lake at the foot of the mountain for half a century, but when a series of small earthquakes started to shake Mount St. Helens in March of 1980, he stepped into the national spotlight for the final two months of his life. As the warning signs grew in intensity and frequency, sheriff's deputies ordered everyone living on the mountain to leave. But Truman was having none of it.

"You couldn't pull me out with a mule team," he boasted to reporters who put themselves in harm's way in search of colourful quotes. "That mountain's part of Truman, and Truman's part of that mountain."

The story of the stubborn old mountain man who refused to leave his home resonated deeply with many Americans, and Truman became a folk hero. He spoke to countless reporters, often sipping his trademark drink, whiskey and Coke, at the same time, profanities peppering his comments. Photos of the rosy-cheeked octogenarian in a green John Deere cap appeared in major publications, and a helicopter flew him to a school in Brooks, Oregon, to answer questions and sign autographs.

His refusal to leave irritated local authorities and no doubt seemed strange to many nervous city dwellers. Truman had built a vacation resort in the idyllic location, nearly a thousand metres above sea level, in the late 1920s. He was not about to leave his home of half a century because some scientists he didn't know told him the volcano might erupt. His wife, Edna, had died three years earlier, and the widower knew he didn't want to spend his last days anywhere else. "I got enough food and liquor to stand a hell of a siege," he said, and he was confident an eruption wouldn't affect him. "I've walked that mountain for fifty years. I know her. If it erupts with lava it's not going to get me at Spirit Lake."

While Truman was enjoying his moment in the spotlight, the north face of Mount St. Helens was starting to bulge. State officials tried to convince Harry Truman to leave one last time. When he refused they left him alone, except for the company of his sixteen cats.

Mount St. Helens is only about thirty-seven thousand years old, which is relatively young as volcanoes go, and has rumbled to life several times over the millenia. The Indigenous people of the area, the Klickitat, were aware of its explosive potential: they called it Louwala-Clough, or Fire Mountain. An eruption in 1900 BCE was likely larger in volume than the infamous eruption of Mount Vesuvius.

If Harry Truman was the stubborn voice of folk wisdom, then David Johnston was the urgent voice of science and safety. The thirty-year-old volcanologist was one of the first members of the US Geological Survey's monitoring team to arrive at Mount St. Helens, and he recognized the deadly risk the mountain posed almost immediately. Johnston was the scientist in charge of studying volcanic gases, and as a result he spent a lot of time working on or near the volcano. Despite his youth, he had considerable experience with volcanoes in Alaska, and he had seen firsthand the explosive potential of one of nature's most terrifying forces when, in 1976, he was studying the uninhabited island volcano of Augustine in the days before it erupted. Johnston and his colleagues were stranded on the slopes of the volcano for several days as high winds grounded their helicopters. They were rescued just twelve hours before Augustine erupted. Johnston's near-miss in Alaska left an indelible impression on him, and he saw a similar threat in Mount St. Helens. "I am genuinely afraid of it," he told reporters.

The US Geological Survey had hired Johnston two years earlier to expand volcano monitoring in Alaska and the Pacific Northwest. His measurements on Mount St. Helens convinced him the threat of a major eruption put thousands of lives at risk. Johnston was instrumental in convincing local authorities that people needed to move out of the surrounding area, and they needed to stay out, even when some impatient local residents started clamouring for the evacuation order to be lifted. And, like other volcanologists, he put himself directly in harm's way, arguing the only accurate way to measure the risk was for scientists like him to be close to that risk. In the weeks before the eruption, as local residents moved away from the mountain, Johnston walked down into the crater to collect samples. He made the dangers clear to any reporters who stepped into the danger zone with him. "We're standing next to a dynamite keg and the fuse is lit," he told them. "We just don't know how long the fuse is."

When the fuse finally ran out, Johnston was standing on a rocky ridge ten kilometres from Mount St. Helens, at a monitoring station named Coldwater II, watching the bulging north face through his binoculars. At 8:31 a.m. on Sunday, May 18, he radioed his colleagues at a makeshift command post in an old US Forest Service building in Vancouver, Washington. "Vancouver! Vancouver!" he barked. "This is it!"

A magnitude-5.1 earthquake triggered a massive slide along the north face of Mount St. Helens. Nearly four hundred metres of the mountain's conical top gave way and hurtled downhill in the largest landslide ever recorded. But more was to come. The collapse of the north face released a pressure cooker of superheated gas and magma, which then exploded in a gigantic lateral blast. A cataclysmic wall of boulders, ash, and gas thundered at near supersonic speed away from the volcano and across the ridge that David Johnston was standing on. He was blown off the ridge, and his body was never found.

The lateral blast burned and flattened roughly six hundred square kilometres of dense forest. On the shores of Spirit Lake, Harry Truman didn't have a chance. Through a telescope twenty kilometres away, a fireman named Fred Johns, from the nearby town of Kelso, saw the massive cloud of ash and superheated gas burst out of the crater and a tremendous avalanche of snow, mud, and ice sweep down the mountainside. "When I saw that big slide hit, I said to myself, if Harry Truman and his sixteen cats were alive in that lodge, they aren't now." He was right: Truman's lodge was buried in fifty metres of debris, as were twenty summer homes a mile down the valley. Spirit Lake, once a crystal-clear jewel, turned almost instantly into a giant mudhole.

The blast was heard for hundreds of kilometres in all directions. It clearcut great forests to the north in an awe-inspiring explosive wave. Within five kilometres of the summit, the trees disappeared completely. Many more kilometres of trees were permanently bent into a northward lean.

Like many of its nearby cousins up and down the Pacific coast, Mount St. Helens is a stratovolcano. Large and steep, stratovolcanoes are built up over time with alternating layers of lava and ash. They're known for their high gas content and as a result produce explosive eruptions. In that sense they differ from shield volcanoes, like Mauna Loa and Kilauea in Hawaii, which have more gentle slopes and milder eruptions. (Of course, shield volcanoes can be highly disruptive as well, as evidenced by the hundreds of homes that were destroyed by the Kilauea eruptions in 2018.) The key difference between shield volcanoes and stratovolcanoes, from a public safety perspective, is that while many can walk away from a slow-moving lava stream (Kilauea claimed no lives in 2018), no one can outrun a pyroclastic flow.

In 1980, as Mount St. Helens let loose at full force, the nearby Toutle River became a conduit for the volcano's destruction. It acted as a deadly downhill freeway for a landslide of volcanic debris called a lahar. The word *lahar* comes from the Indonesian island of Java, which lies in the middle of a belt of dozens of volcanoes. Lahars are one of the deadliest aspects of stratovolcanoes, because the snow and ice near the eruption tend to melt quickly and mix with the pyroclastic flow, letting it move farther and faster than it would otherwise. The Toutle River swelled into a steaming torrent within minutes. The first of several lahars tore down the river valley, cutting new channels through the forest on either side of the river with ease and adding even more freshly uprooted trees to the already clogged river. The fast-moving wall of water and trees mixed with volcanic ash and smashed into Camp Baker, a Weyerhaeuser logging operation west of the volcano. Three people at the camp drowned; volcanic rock and ash fatally burned two others.

One of the many remarkable things about the blast was the differences in what people heard depending on where they were located. The boom was heard in southern British Columbia, more than four hundred kilometres away, but many survivors who were close to the mountain said they didn't hear a thing. The silence may have been a factor of the topography, the wind, and the temperature differences between altitudes. Whatever the reason, the disconnect between the visual devastation and the lack of noise was surreal for people looking up at Mount St. Helens from below. They certainly felt the blast, though, and the rapidly changing air around them. Some survivors described the air feeling electric and their hair standing straight on end.

Not long after the lateral blast, a second explosion sent a column of ash shooting twenty-two or twenty-three kilometres straight up before drifting east. The fifty thousand people who lived in the town of Yakima, more than 130 kilometres away, were in total darkness by lunch. Up to fifteen centimetres of ash covered communities across eastern Washington. A horseshoe-shaped crater was left where Mount St. Helens's beautifully symmetrical conical peak had been.

The blast, while spectacular, was but a fraction of the largest known volcanic eruption in recorded human history, the 1815 eruption of Mount Tambora, on the Indonesian island of Sumbawa. Tambora resulted in the deaths of tens of thousands of people, some dying in the blast itself and others in the famine that followed. The US Geological Survey estimates the Mount Tambora blast produced thirty to eighty times more ash than the 1980 Mount St. Helens eruption. Some prehistoric blasts were likely even stronger. Mount St. Helens killed fifty-seven people in 1980 and caused more than a billion dollars in damage. The loss of life could have been much worse if authorities hadn't heeded the advice of David Johnston and other scientists, and the financial cost would have been much higher if the eruption had happened closer to a major city. Scientists still monitor Mount St. Helens, watching for signs it may rumble back to life. They watch other volcanoes closely, too, including a bigger mountain, eighty kilometres north of Mount St. Helens, that may pose an even greater risk.

Rising 4,392 metres above sea level, Mount Rainier is an icon of the Pacific Northwest: a near-constant presence on the horizon for millions of people and the namesake for a range of commercial ventures and places, from beaches to bullets to beer. Rainier is the most glaciated peak in the lower forty-eight states, capped by vast slopes of snow and twenty-five glaciers. On clear days people in Portland, Oregon, can see it looming above the lower western slopes of Mount St. Helens, and it can even be visible in the Victoria, BC, suburb of Oak Bay. On occasion, Rainier's white peak looks to be floating above the clouds. Despite its ethereal appearance, however, Mount Rainier is one of the most dangerous volcanoes in North America.

The volcano has been active for about half a million years. Its most recent lava flow was about 2,200 years ago, and its last pyroclastic flows about 1,100 years ago. (Geologists have not found evidence to support vague reports of small eruptions in the nineteenth century.) Like other volcanoes, Rainier spews gas, ash, and lava, but what really makes emergency planners nervous is the threat of deadly lahars flowing into highly populated areas. These volcanic mudflows have swept down the White River to the lowlands around Puget Sound about half a dozen times over the last six thousand years. If that happened today, hundreds of thousands of people could be at risk. The Cascades Volcano Observatory estimates a lahar from Mount Rainier could reach larger communities in as little as forty-five minutes.

As the scientist in charge of the Cascades Volcano Observatory, Seth Moran takes the risk to public safety seriously. The eruption of Mount Rainier 5,600 years ago offers an especially chilling warning. A massive collapse on the peak of the volcano created a horseshoe-shaped crater like the one on Mount St. Helens. It also unleashed what is now known as the Osceola Mudflow, a lahar that swept down different forks of the White River all the way to Puget Sound. The lahar would have resembled a massive wall of liquid cement, 150 metres deep in some stretches, travelling at about twenty-five kilometres an hour and sweeping up rocks, trees, and anything else in its path. The lahar covered an area of about 550 square kilometres, stretching into what is now the Seattle suburb of Kent and the Port of Tacoma. It dried quickly and now forms the bedrock under Tacoma, more than sixty kilometres from Rainier's summit. Geologists have compared the chemistry of the rocks back up the path from Tacoma to the summit and confirmed they are from the same event. That is more than an academic exercise. It is crucial for public safety to know how far deadly volcanic mudflows have reached in the past, and how far they may reach again in the future.

The implications of the Osceola Mudflow are terrifying: more than two hundred thousand people live right on top of the path of destruction it cut 5,600 years ago. Scientists are quick to point out the next major eruption and lahar could be decades, even centuries, away. But, as is the case with both earthquakes and tsunamis, they insist this natural disaster could come soon, and communities in its path need to prepare. History shows what can happen if they don't.

Nevado del Ruiz is an active stratovolcano with a history of producing dangerous lahars. The glacier-capped giant stands in Colombia, close to the equator, and its nearly 5,400-metre peak is the northernmost in the Andean volcanic belt. The Spanish word *nevado* means snow-capped and is a fitting title for a volcano that is covered in about twenty-five square kilometres of snow and ice. Nevado del Ruiz has a long history of eruptions and lahars, including several since the Spanish colonized the area. In 1595 a lahar killed 636 people. In 1845 a giant lahar flowed down Lagunillas River before flooding the valley floor, seventy kilometres downstream, and killing more than a thousand. Worse was to come. In the years following the 1845 lahar, the village of Armero was built on top of the mudflow in the lower valley of the Lagunillas River. The little village grew, and by 1985 it was home to more than twenty-seven thousand people.

The residents of Armero were aware of the volcano looming above them. If its deadly history wasn't enough to cause concern, several months of minor earthquakes and steam explosions had put many people in the town on edge by the spring of 1985. But worrying is one thing. Ordering the evacuation of twenty-seven thousand people is another thing entirely.

Colombia lacked both the volcano-monitoring equipment that the US Geological Survey had used on Mount St. Helens and the trained geologists. The government flew in magma-monitoring seismographs from overseas and set them up near the summit, and a report completed in early October 1985 concluded that a moderate eruption would produce a "100 per cent probability of mudflows...with great danger for Armero" and surrounding villages. Few copies were printed, however, and nervous Colombian officials chose not to evacuate. A steady stream of tremors started on November 10, and a group of geologists visited the crater on November 12. They were not convinced an eruption was imminent; they were proved catastrophically wrong the very next day.

The volcano erupted in the afternoon of November 13, showering pumice fragments and ash on Armero. Community leaders urged calm, but the Red Cross ordered an evacuation at 7 p.m., an order that was lifted almost immediately because the ash stopped falling. A little after nine o'clock a more serious eruption occurred. This time the volcano ejected molten rock and pyroclastic flows that rapidly started to melt the ice cap. If the skies had been clear, residents of Armero might have noticed the deadly explosion above them. But a storm was passing through, obscuring their view of the summit. Meltwater and hot pyroclastic flows mixed together to produce a series of deadly lahars. One of those volcanic mudflows swept down the Cauca River Valley, swamping the village of Chinchiná and killing 1,927 people. Another deadly lahar sped down the Lagunillas River, the same path of the two previous tragedies. The largest lahar reached speeds of fifty kilometres per hour. It broke through a natural dam and reached Armero two hours later.

The first blow to the town was a wall of water, a product of the broken dam. Ten minutes later, hot, thick volcanic mud smashed into and over Armero. More than three-quarters of the people were killed within twenty minutes, swept away or submerged in liquid death. In total, more than twenty-three thousand people died in the deadly lahars from Nevado del Ruiz.

At a mass funeral in the state capital, Ibagué, a banner in the crowd expressed the popular verdict of Colombians: "The Volcano didn't kill 22,000 people. The Government Killed Them." Angry survivors demanded the resignation of the provincial governor and several federal ministers. While the government felt intense pressure to account for the appalling loss of life, the Armero tragedy was not its only crisis. Violence tied to drug cartels was endemic. Just a week before the volcano erupted, Marxist rebels had stormed the country's Palace of Justice and held the Supreme Court hostage. When the Colombian military recaptured the building, nearly half of the judges were killed.

Some local officials had done their best to prepare. Ramon Antonio Rodriguez-Robayo, the mayor of Armero, had recognized that a time bomb loomed above his hometown. He tried to persuade officials at higher levels of government to act for months, but his concerns were routinely dismissed. The possibility of floods if an eruption burst the natural dam upstream from Armero troubled the mayor. Eventually, he persuaded a congressman to quiz the ministers of mines, public works, and defence about the mayor's concerns. All of them claimed the Colombian government was aware of the risk and was acting to protect the local population. Rodriguez-Robayo wanted the government to dismantle the upstream dam, but that did not happen. He continued to pressure the provincial governor, who eventually refused to talk to the persistent mayor. Despite his fears, Rodriguez-Robayo refused to leave Armero, and he tried to save his people until the end. He died pleading for help through an amateur radio operator's transmitter and was buried in volcanic mud along with the people he was trying to protect.

Volcanic mudflows are especially unforgiving natural disasters. Other types of disasters typically injure more people than they kill. The Nevado del Ruiz catastrophe killed four times as many people as it injured. Many of those who initially survived and were injured and trapped faced a much more protracted death. The scale of the catastrophe convinced Colombian officials that few people could have survived, so they were slow to mount an organized rescue effort. Foreign diplomats and the Red Cross complained that the military stymied their efforts; the military blamed the vast stretch of thick mud for slowing the search. A few dozen helicopters from Colombia and a handful of other countries searched from the skies. But, the *New York Times* reported, it took five days for Colombian firefighters to cut the roofs off the few buildings that survived the mudslide, despite reports of survivors crying for help from inside.

When rescuers did reach buried victims, they often found desperate people buried so inextricably as to be almost assured a slow and painful death. In many cases rescuers could only offer some food and medicine or pray with the victims before they died. The best-known victim was thirteen-year-old Omayra Sanchez. Trapped in the concrete and brick debris of her home, submerged in mud up to her shoulders for sixty hours, the stoic girl maintained a composure and dignity that captured the hearts of volunteer rescuers and journalists who came to interview her. A few hours before she died, French photographer Frank Fournier captured a heartbreaking photograph of Omayra, gazing steadily at the camera's lens. For many people in Colombia and around the world, the photograph of Omayra Sanchez came to symbolize both the devastation that nature can unleash and the human inaction that can make it so much more deadly.

Nevado del Ruiz, Mount Rainier, and Mount St. Helens are just faces in the volcanic crowd. Around the world are approximately 1,500 potentially active volcanoes, three quarters of them in the Ring of Fire, where four of the five deadliest eruptions ever recorded have occurred. This seismically active ring stretches north from New Zealand, boomerangs to the west under Indonesia, veers northeast under the Philippines and Japan, continues up to Kamchatka, curves under the Aleutian Islands to Alaska, and carries on down the west coasts of North and South America.

Mount Baker, like Mount St. Helens and Mount Rainier, is in Washington State. It's near the Canadian border and easily visible in cities like Abbotsford, Vancouver, and Victoria, and its stunning snow-capped peak occupies a similarly iconic space on the horizon for people in southwestern British Columbia as Mount Rainier does for people in and around Seattle. But Mount Baker is also a threat, and it could be a big one for people in southern British Columbia. The volcano's deadly lahars could reach all the way to Abbotsford and its 150,000 residents.

Mount Baker erupted in 1843, resulting in the death of a lot of fish, a forest fire, and the spreading of volcanic ash. It erupted again in 1880, and it released steam without erupting in the mid-1970s. Over the last ten thousand years, the majestic stratovolcano has produced eight lahars, and a few of those have reached into what are now heavily populated areas. Natural Resources Canada estimates that lahars big enough to reach Abbotsford happen once every fourteen thousand years. Scientists at the agency are quick to point out that weather-related floods in the area are much more common. That is in large part why Mount Rainier is considered a much bigger threat to human life than Mount Baker.

In Tacoma, some people have planned an escape route in case Mount Rainier ever sends a lahar steaming down the river valleys. If that seems overly cautious to some, it's certainly not crazy. After all, Mount Rainier has erupted as recently as the 1800s and could do so again in our lifetime. Other geological catastrophes are so infrequent, however, that it could be argued most of us shouldn't worry too much about them. Take the Yellowstone Caldera in Yellowstone National Park in Wyoming. Supervolcanoes like Yellowstone have the potential to change the world's climate. In fact, some scientists believe a major eruption of Yellowstone could kill millions of people, because a huge volume of ash spread across a swath of North America's farmland will inevitably cause a famine. But the US Geological Survey calculates the probability of that happening in any given year at roughly one in 730,000, roughly the odds of a large asteroid hitting Earth. Yellowstone is likely to cause steam explosions and some earthquakes but nothing as bad as the cataclysmic eruption that happened 2.1 million years ago.

Yellowstone shouldn't keep us awake at night, but it shouldn't be ignored by scientists, either. Geological events do not follow strict schedules, and predictions are not infallible. Volcanoes provide warnings ahead of time, and scientists need to be listening.

Chapter 5

CALIFORNIA DREAMING

Tens of millions of baseball fans turned on their televisions to watch Game 3 of the World Series on October 17, 1989. It featured the neighbouring San Francisco Giants and Oakland Athletics and was billed as the Bay Bridge Series.

The opening pitch was scheduled for 5:35 p.m. at Candlestick Park, and thousands of fans were already in the stands at 5:04. ABC broadcaster Tim McCarver was just starting his pre-game analysis when the video feed cut out, and anchor Al Michaels was heard in the background saying, "We're having an earth—." The sound went dead, but the ABC broadcast team acted quickly and in just five seconds put a green "ABC World Series" banner on the screen. In another fifteen seconds, Michaels's voice came back. "I don't know if we're on the air or not, and I'm not sure I care at this particular moment," he said. "But we are! Well, folks, that's the greatest opening in the history of television—bar none!"

The magnitude-6.9 quake had lasted fifteen seconds at most, but that was more than enough time for the tens of thousands of fans in the park. Those who were standing in line for beer and food or making their way to their seats saw and felt waves roll through the concrete floors of the concourse as though it was made of water. The power went out, and many people started screaming. Millions of TV viewers could hear them in the background as Al Michaels threw to a commercial break. "And we will be back—we hope—from San Francisco, in just a moment!"

Outside the stadium, matters were much more serious. People in tall towers felt the floors sway frighteningly, and office cabinets crab-walked across rooms. On the streets, people clung to parking meters, signposts, or anything else they could wrap their arms around to stop themselves from being thrown to the ground. Drivers on freeways thought their cars were having all sorts of mechanical issues, from cracked axels to temperamental transmissions. One Santa Cruz resident saw telephone poles snapping back and forth like windshield wipers.

Will Horter had left work early to watch the ball game. He took the BART train from his office in downtown San Francisco to West Oakland, the first stop on the Oakland side of the bay. Horter and his girlfriend lived in the main-floor apartment of an old Victorian house that stood a block away from the Cypress Freeway Viaduct, California's first elevated double-deck highway, which had loomed over the poor inner-city neighbourhood since the 1950s. Horter got home a few minutes after his girlfriend, who was on the couch, watching TV. The moment he opened the door, the shaking started.

"Her eyes grew really big," Horter recalls, "and she just jumped up and grabbed me in a bear hug, and then everything started flying around. I had a brick shelf. Well, that went down right away. Then we heard this huge bang from upstairs."

The elderly couple that owned the house lived in a separate suite on the top floor. They had an extensive library of books stored in milk crates, which crashed down and were responsible for the bang Horter heard. When the shaking stopped, the house was still standing, but it was bent and damaged significantly. The walls were twisted enough that some doors were difficult to open. Others were simply jammed shut. Horter's landlords were trapped, so he found a chainsaw and used it to cut into the wall studs so he could open their door. Then he stepped outside to look at the damage on his block. It took him a few seconds to realize what he was looking at. "It was very weird, because if you just casually looked at them, they looked like a [one-storey] house," he said. "They were two-storey houses that became one-storey houses." West Oakland was largely built on fill, and the unstable nature of that soft soil amplified the shaking and proved too much for many houses. Some sank, others collapsed, and rescue efforts started almost immediately after the shaking stopped.

Horter went back home to find a wrench. He was recovering from a serious back injury, but he walked as quickly as he could from house to house, using the wrench to turn off every gas meter he could find. Desperate cries coming from the elevated freeway at the end of the block caught his attention. "People were screaming, 'They got crushed in the earthquake!'" Horter ran to the freeway and found a scene that would haunt many commuters and transportation planners for years to come. Vertical support columns had buckled outwards, causing the upper deck to collapse onto the lower one, crushing cars as if they were tin cans.

Horter was one of the first people to show up at the scene. Though his back injury prevented him from climbing, he helped other locals who used ladders to clamber into the wreckage. Police officers soon arrived and, mistaking some black rescuers for looters, tried to arrest them. "We said, 'No, they're saving people!'" he remembered.

Some of those trapped in the rubble were saved, but forty-two others lost their lives in the Cypress Freeway Viaduct collapse. That number would almost certainly have been much higher if the normal rush-hour traffic had been on the road at the time, but traffic was light because so many baseball fans had left work early to watch the game. Buck Helm, a fifty-seven-year-old longshoreman, was still trapped on October 21, four days later, when an engineer inspecting the damage found him. A large beam from the freeway's structure had fallen in front of Helm's car and prevented the upper vehicle deck from crushing it completely. When he was finally taken to the hospital, he was diagnosed with a skull fracture, three broken ribs, nerve damage, and severe dehydration. Local radio stations referred to him as Lucky Buck, and he survived for more than a month in two different hospitals, living to see his fifty-eighth birthday, before dying of respiratory failure soon after. Helm's death was the sixty-seventh overall in what would come to be known as the Loma Prieta Earthquake.

A segment of the San Francisco–Oakland Bay Bridge road deck fell onto the lower deck, after bolts holding it in place sheared off in the shaking. No one was killed when it fell, but one driver on the upper deck who didn't see the deadly gap in time was killed when she drove into it. The Embarcadero, a double-deck freeway on the other side of the bay in San Francisco, also suffered serious damage that forced the closure of an important connection between the Golden Gate Bridge and Bay Bridge. (It also reignited a long-simmering debate over whether the freeway, a "hideous monstrosity" according to the editorial board of the *San Francisco Chronicle* that, like the Alaskan Way Viaduct in Seattle, separated much of downtown from the water, should be repaired or simply torn down.)

While the elevated freeways and the Bay Bridge made headlines, transportation planners had a lot more to worry about. Governor George Deukmejian ordered a review of twelve thousand bridges across California. What the engineers found wasn't comforting. Many older overpasses were considered vulnerable to collapse because they rested on strings of isolated support columns rather than the more robust clusters of columns found under newer bridges. The engineers also pointed to the need for stronger joints under freeway decks. Finally, they focused on the complicated relationship between bridge structures and the ground they rest on, noting the section of the Cypress Freeway Viaduct that collapsed was built on fill while the adjoining sections that remained standing were on more solid ground.

With new knowledge—and fear—California started the tall task of retrofitting thousands of bridge structures. The state also added seismic instruments to measure the shaking that bridges endure in quakes, thereby helping engineers make important decisions about whether bridges can be reopened safely after a quake. California was determined to learn from the disaster and make the state safer in the future. In the meantime, life gradually returned to normal. The World Series resumed ten days after the dramatic interruption, the Athletics sweeping the Giants in four games. Many still remember the 1989 matchup as the Earthquake Series, but it isn't the only reason San Francisco, more than any other city, is associated with earthquakes.

In the twilight of the morning of April 18, 1906, the ground under San Francisco jolted suddenly and then stood still. It was twelve minutes after five o'clock, and though some of the city's four hundred thousand residents noticed the tremor, most were still asleep. They were awoken less than thirty seconds later, when the ground started to shake violently.

The shaking lasted almost a minute and brought one of the world's most dynamic cities to its knees. Terrified people rushed into the streets in bare feet and nightgowns. The psychologist William James recalled being thrown to the floor, the earth "shaking the room exactly as a terrier shakes a rat." Horses bolted and galloped through the chaos. Panic-stricken dogs sprinted away from the city, whimpering and panting their way up the surrounding hills. The tenor Enrico Caruso, who had performed in *Carmen* the night before at the Mission Opera House, was asleep on the fifth floor of the Palace Hotel when the quake struck. He woke up to find his bed rocking as though he were on a ship on the ocean and looked out his window to "see the buildings toppling over, big pieces of masonry falling, and from the street below I hear cries and screams."

The US Geological Survey now estimates the quake was magnitude 7.9. It occurred along the famous San Andreas fault: the geological boundary that splits much of California in two and separates the Pacific plate from the North American plate. The San Andreas fault ruptured along a 476-kilometre stretch, from somewhere near the city of San Juan Bautista all the way up to Cape Mendocino, where the fault meets the Cascadia Subduction Zone. The shaking was felt from Los Angeles to Oregon to Nevada. But San Francisco suffered the most, both because of its proximity to the San Andreas fault and because this was a shallow earthquake, only eight kilometres beneath the surface.

"EARTHQUAKE AND FIRE: SAN FRANCISCO IN RUINS" was the headline at the top of the combined *Call-Chronicle-Examiner* newspaper the day after the quake. Reporters and editors at all three papers worked through the aftershocks to put out the four-page edition. Even as the news was written and printed, bodies were being pulled from the rubble, and fires, the result of ruptured gas lines, were spreading across the city. "Death and destruction have been the fate of San Francisco," the paper declared. "Downtown everything is in ruin. Not a business house stands. Theatres are crumbled into heaps. Factories and commission houses lie smouldering on their former sites.... On every side there was death and suffering yesterday. Hundreds were injured, either burned, crushed, or struck by falling pieces from the buildings."

Broken bricks, snapped timber frames, shattered windows, bent steel girders, and cracked decorative stone clogged city streets. Tangled electrical wire draped over the piles of debris, smoke, and flames made the wreckage worse. Many downtown residents felt trapped. They believed, incorrectly, that the wharves had burned and the ferries had stopped running. As a result, many thought their only hope of survival was to reach the west side of Van Ness Avenue and possibly the sand dunes of Golden Gate Park and the Presidio. The writer and women's rights advocate Louise Herrick Wall walked among San Francisco's burning buildings in the hours and days that followed the quake. She believed thousands could have escaped across San Francisco Bay if they had only known it was possible. "The city to them was a trap with the only one possible egress, miles and miles to the west," she wrote. "Day after day and all night long, without regular food, drink, rest, or respite from intense anxiety, thousands of families of women and little children dragged themselves from place to place in front of the flames, lying without shelter in vacant lots, exposed to fog and chilling rain. Premature childbirth and death to the feeblest of the old people resulted from the fatal misconception."

The fires burned and the death toll climbed for four days. By the time rain finally extinguished the flames, almost five hundred city blocks had been burned or razed, more than three thousand brick buildings had collapsed, and more than twenty-four thousand wood buildings were lost. At the time, the US Army recorded just 664 deaths in and around San Francisco, San Jose, and Santa Rosa; later studies suggested the number was closer to three thousand. Of those who survived, more than two hundred thousand were left homeless.

The disaster would have been the end of some cities. But not San Francisco. The economic forces that had built the great metropolis fuelled a remarkable rebirth. Reconstruction efforts started almost immediately. But in the rush to rebuild, San Francisco repeated some of the same mistakes it had made in the first place: erecting unreinforced brick buildings that could collapse in another earthquake and wooden houses that could burn down in another conflagration. The city also built over soft marshland and on top of rubble from buildings destroyed in the earthquake. But one important aspect of San Francisco's resurrection was a serious safety improvement: firefighting. By 1912 San Francisco had built a new auxiliary water-supply system to dramatically improve the city's ability to stop fire from spreading in the future. Thanks to a new network of reservoirs, cisterns, and pipes, firefighters had access to much more water. The city also bought fireboats and built pumping stations that could pump sea water to douse the flames. The auxiliary water-supply system made San Francisco safer, and it also established California's pattern of learning important lessons from past earthquakes.

The Long Beach earthquake of 1933 shook the Los Angeles area late on a Friday afternoon, just before six o'clock. The shallow earthquake rumbled up from under the ocean floor, along the Newport-Inglewood fault. The 6.4-magnitude quake collapsed several buildings. Water tanks fell off roofs and masonry cornices and chimney bricks rained down on roads and sidewalks. One hundred and twenty people died in the disaster, but again timing was everything. More than 230 schools either collapsed or were seriously damaged, and if the quake had happened during school hours many children would have lost their lives.

The near miss convinced California lawmakers to act. State Assemblyman Don Field lived in the city of Glendale, about fifty kilometres from Long Beach. He'd worked as a building contractor before entering politics, and the damage he saw deeply disturbed him. Field knew buildings could be made safer, so he returned to the state capital of Sacramento and met with the state architect, George McDougall, and an engineer named WC Willett. Within days, they'd drafted a bill that would make new schools in California much safer. The bill required all new schools to be built by a licensed structural engineer. It also required approval and inspection by the Division of the State Architect. The bill promised to improve the odds of survival for students in a future quake, but it applied only to new construction; it would not make existing schools safer.

The bill was submitted as emergency legislation to the California Assembly less than two weeks after the quake and passed with unanimous approval. Then state senators, suspicious of the quick progress of the bill, spent a few weeks taking a close look before approving it. On April 10, a month to the day after the earthquake, Governor James Rolph signed the Field Act into law. Some observers argued the bill received bipartisan support because the tragic consequences of Earth's terrifying power were so fresh in legislators' minds. The Long Beach quake wouldn't be the last disaster to claim lives and then prompt lifesaving changes.

In 1971 the San Fernando earthquake focused public concern on freeways. The magnitude-6.6 shock was felt across the heavily populated Greater Los Angeles area. Of the eight million residents, roughly two million experienced moderate shaking for eight to twelve seconds, and four hundred thousand felt very strong ground-shaking. Of the fifty-nine people who died, only two were killed by collapsing freeway infrastructure. But once again, this was largely the result of timing: the earthquake occurred at 6 a.m. when few cars were on the road. Twelve freeway overpasses collapsed, sending chills up the spines of drivers and transportation planners alike in a state built around the automobile.

The California Department of Transportation, CalTrans, responded with new design criteria for bridges and highway infrastructure to make them more robust. Before 1971, specific seismic provisions for bridges and highways didn't exist, because it was presumed that earthquakes couldn't put as much of a load on an overpass as day-to-day stresses like heavy traffic and wind. The twelve collapses proved otherwise, and CalTrans changed the standards to demand stronger overpasses. It also initiated a seismic-safety retrofit program to bring old bridges up to the new standards. But California had thousands of bridges, most of which ended up waiting in line, like so many cars on state freeways. While the state had learned important lessons from the earthquake and made improvements to some overpasses in response, it left many other needed improvements undone.

The 1971 San Fernando quake also exposed dangerous vulnerabilities in buildings. Most of the victims were inside one wing of the San Fernando Veterans Administration Hospital. That wing was built with unreinforced concrete in 1926 and could not withstand the shaking. Nurse Betty Van Decar had just finished a night shift at the hospital when Ward 5 collapsed. "It buckled down, caved in, the whole building," she recalled. "There was an awful sound. You could hear the ground rumbling. I thought, they're not going to make it." Forty-six people died in the collapse and several other hospitals were damaged, a few knocked out of service at the precise moment they were needed most. "The lesson is clear," a team of researchers from the California Institute of Technology concluded, "that certain structures should be designed to be stronger than the minimum requirements of the building code." Some standards were improved after 1971, but as was the case with freeway overpasses, many remained vulnerable, as Californians learned in San Francisco and Oakland in 1989 and again in a quake near Los Angeles five years after that.

The San Fernando Valley shook on January 17, Martin Luther King Day, 1994. The epicentre of the Northridge earthquake was in Reseda, the Los Angeles suburb made famous by Tom Petty in his song "Free Fallin'." Like the 1989 San Francisco quake, this temblor was short and violent, lasting just ten to twenty seconds, but it was the most damaging quake in and around Los Angeles since 1971. Although both quakes were a similar magnitude, the Northridge quake arguably made a greater impression on engineers because of the intense ground forces. Scientists had placed hundreds of scientific instruments on buildings, bridges, and dams around the region, and as a result they collected more data from the Northridge earthquake than any before it. The information was extensive and frightening, showing some of the highest accelerations and velocities ever recorded. To make matters worse, this immense force emanated from a previously unknown fault.

The sudden ground accelerations proved too much for some key pieces of infrastructure. Once again, freeways fared badly. A police officer was killed when he drove his motorcycle off a collapsed portion of freeway interchange. The interchange had been rebuilt to a higher seismic standard in the 1970s, but the Northridge earthquake proved that standard still wasn't high enough. Some of the most startling images of the Northridge quake are of shattered freeway columns pointing skyward, with bent jumbles of twisted rebar, the rubble of the roadways they once supported, piled around them. America's busiest road, the Santa Monica Freeway, suffered serious damage to its bridges and connectors. This would be problematic in any city, but in a metropolis where three million cars clog the roads every day, it could have meant chaos. Local officials cut red tape and repair crews worked round the clock to reopen the crucial route three months after it crumbled.

Images of fallen freeways caught the world's attention, but the Northridge quake shook out other deadly deficiencies. Despite all the old unreinforced masonry, vulnerable bridges, and shaky freeway underpinnings in Los Angeles, a three-storey wood apartment complex proved the deadliest. Fifty-seven people were killed in the Northridge quake, and the highest single death toll was recorded at an unassuming apartment building called Northridge Meadows, where sixteen people lost their lives. Most of the 163 apartments were located on the upper two floors of the building. Those upper floors were relatively sturdy, but the ground floor was not. It was what is known as a soft storey, which lacks the strength of the floors above it. The ground floor was weak because it included many open parking spaces for cars. Instead of continuous walls, much of the ground-floor perimeter of the building consisted of single steel posts, which have much less lateral resistance. When the shaking started, the steel posts toppled within seconds, and as a result, much of the upper two-thirds of the building pancaked down on the ground floor, crushing forty apartments and trapping sleeping residents in their beds.

When firefighters arrived, they found what looked like a two-storey building that had suffered only minor damage. But when they walked around the side, they realized what had happened. Residents of the upper floors were crouching and peering into the dark voids under the collapsed structure. Firefighters called for support, but none was available; other units were responding to emergencies elsewhere. Some firefighters and bystanders considered crawling into the tight confines of the collapsed ground floor, but that was a serious safety risk because of aftershocks and possible settling. Once firefighters had ensured that all of the upper floors were empty, they started the arduous task of cutting through the floor of the second storey to try to access people trapped below. This proved to be a lot harder than it might sound. The inch-thick plywood floor was coated in a two-inch-thick layer of concrete, and rested on top of two-inch-by-twelve-inch vertical floor joists. But by the middle of the afternoon, they had pulled twenty-five survivors out of the wreckage.

The disaster at Northridge Meadows was a dramatic illustration of the dangers of ground-level soft storeys. The death toll this relatively small building caused was an eye-opener for Californians. Many similar buildings could be found all over the state, and many people could now imagine themselves trapped. Concern over soft-storey buildings rose steadily in the years that followed, and various levels of government took modest steps to improve safety. Roughly 1,500 concrete and 13,500 wood buildings in Los Angeles were identified as being at high risk of collapse; the daunting numbers were likely one of the reasons so little was done to address this risk for so long. Many owners of concrete-frame buildings had long downplayed the risk, arguing their buildings had withstood past quakes and were built with some steel reinforcing bar inside their concrete frames. But that limited steel reinforcement can bend during heavy shaking, and some concrete columns could blow out altogether and collapse.

Despite significant challenges and costs, Los Angeles City Council voted unanimously in favour of a municipal ordinance that would require the retrofit of both pre-1978 wood-frame soft-storey buildings and non-ductile concrete buildings. "We finally took our head out of the sand," Mayor Eric Garcetti said. The plan faced opposition. While many now agreed with the need for retrofits, they questioned whether building owners and tenants should have to pay for them. Owners of wood apartment buildings faced retrofit bills of $100,000 or more. Fixes for some concrete buildings topped $1 million, with a few owners needing to pay six figures just to have the building assessed.

The city offered owners more time in an effort to ease some of the financial burden. Those who owned wood apartment buildings were given seven years to finish the work. Owners of concrete buildings were given three years to have their building assessed, ten years to submit retrofit plans, and twenty-five years to finish the work. The city also allowed landlords to increase rents by as much as $75 a month, although it later considered cutting that number in half in response to concerns that many people would be priced out of their homes. Some landlords suggested the costs would be too great to cover, even with rent increases, and speculated their buildings would simply have to be torn down.

San Francisco has tried similar measures. The city identified nearly five thousand multi-unit houses and apartments with ground floors that included large, open spaces like convenience stores, or basements with parking garages. In some cases, much of the weight of the upper two or three floors rested on just a few thin posts. In 2013 San Francisco passed a law requiring the buildings' owners to strengthen them. The retrofits varied from building to building but usually included constructing a new shear wall in place of an opening, adding steel frames and bolts, fixing footings, and strengthening the concrete foundation. In 2017 the *San Francisco Chronicle* estimated some wood apartment buildings would need as much as $1 million in work, while smaller buildings might be fixed for closer to $100,000. Deadlines differed depending on the building specifications, but every owner was expected to apply for work permits by September 2018, and all of the work had to be completed within two years. Any building that wasn't upgraded on time would be visited by city building inspectors and would have a large placard, with "EARTHQUAKE WARNING" written across the top in red, displayed at the front of the property. "This building is in violation of the requirements of the San Francisco Code regarding earthquake safety," the signs instructed in English, Spanish, and Chinese. The measure also contained a financial penalty: until they committed to retrofitting the building, the owner of the placarded property would be forbidden from charging tenants rent. As a result, thousands of vulnerable buildings in San Francisco have been strengthened. When the next major earthquake rattles the bay area, the damage will be extensive—but hopefully much less than it would have been without the mandatory retrofit program.

California leads the United States and Canada in earthquake preparation. A 2016 study led by Scott B. Miles, an expert on disaster risk reduction at the University of Washington, concluded California is "the most active state in dealing with earthquake hazards," noting it's the only state with specific policies on unreinforced masonry buildings and requirements for seismic safety in hospitals and schools. California is also the only state with seismic microzonation, which is essentially the detailed mapping of local earthquake hazards such as liquefaction, landslides, and earthquake-triggered flooding. (In 2014 the British Columbia government hired the former director of the California Governor's Office of Emergency Services to assess the province's earthquake preparations. When Henry Renteria came north he found considerable room for improvement, concluding that "the lack of significant seismic activity near highly populated areas has resulted in widespread apathy. This has meant that earthquake preparedness has not received the day-to-day attention that other pressing needs have received.") But for all of California's impressive regulations on brick buildings, vulnerable ground floors, and low-rise concrete buildings, one type of construction could be a towering concern when the next big quake strikes the Golden State.

Steel-frame skyscrapers epitomize the modern American city and look as though their size and modernity must make them relatively earthquake safe. But after the 1994 Northridge quake, when engineers arrived at the Borax corporate headquarters building in Valencia, they were stunned to find the one-year-old structure leaning visibly. Inside, they found cracks in many connections where the building's horizontal steel beams were welded to the vertical steel columns. Later inspection revealed that three quarters of these crucial joints had suffered severe brittle fractures. Other buildings suffered similar damage, including the Getty Museum, which was under construction at the time. The discovery of serious damage in these welded steel-frame buildings astonished engineers. Since 1906, they had placed their faith in the strength of steel frames: when the dust and smoke from the San Francisco earthquake cleared, it revealed roughly two dozen steel-frame towers that survived relatively unscathed. Some of them are still standing today.

Engineers working in California in 1994 describe something close to panic in their ranks following the Northridge quake. They now applied to welded steel-frame buildings the question they'd applied to freeway infrastructure five years earlier: if the structures sustained this much damage in twenty seconds or less, what would happen to them in one of the stronger earthquakes that's expected to strike the state in the coming decades? The 1989 and 1994 quakes were considerably smaller than the one in 1906, which released roughly sixteen times as much energy as the 1989 quake and lasted three to four times as long. When the next 1906-type quake hits, the shaking might not be much stronger, but it is predicted to last up to a minute and shake the ground of a larger area. The extra seconds could collapse buildings and bridges that might withstand shorter tremors. And if fifteen seconds of strong shaking caused a few sections of freeway and bridge decks to collapse, what would a full minute over a larger area do?

That's more than a theoretical concern in downtown San Francisco, where steel-frame skyscrapers dominate the skyline and the former reticence about building extremely high structures in the middle of an active seismic zone seems largely forgotten. Somewhere in the middle of all that steel is the office of a structural engineer named Ronald Hamburger, who has worked on skyscrapers for decades and has the grey hairs to prove it. In 2019 he was hired to work on the fifty-eight-storey, fourteen-year-old Millennium Tower condominium building. The "Leaning Tower of Lawsuits," as *60 Minutes* dubbed it, had sunk forty-three centimetres at ground level and was leaning thirty-five centimetres to the northwest on top. In a city waiting for the next big earthquake, the tilting tower unsettled many. Hamburger devised a plan to install more than fifty piles under the sidewalk beside the building to stabilize it.

Hamburger works out of 100 Pine Place, a thirty-three-storey office tower built in 1972 using the same type of steel construction that now worries engineers. The boardroom in Hamburger's sixteenth-floor office offers an expansive view of several surrounding towers, including the thirty-two-storey Russ Building, a neo-Gothic beauty built in 1927 that stood as the city's tallest building for more than thirty years. Its exterior walls are made of brick and terra cotta tiles, but a steel skeleton of horizontal beams bolted to vertical columns supports the Russ.

Steel-frame tower construction began in the 1800s, Hamburger observes, after Elisha Otis's invention of the safety elevator convinced people they could get up and down without losing their lives or climbing a lot of stairs, and steel beams enabled the building of the first high-rises. Before then, steel was used primarily in the building of railroads, but human ingenuity now started to stretch up rather than out. Chicago and New York raced skyward, and San Francisco got in on the game soon after. When the early steel-frame towers survived the 1906 earthquake, Hamburger said, engineers were convinced that steel frames were earthquake-resistant. Back then, big buildings were composed of horizontal steel beams bolted onto vertical steel columns. Masonry walls filled in the rectangular spaces in between, which added to the strength of the structure, resulting in a very robust tower. But labour costs started to rise after the Second World War, and engineers started to look for more economical ways to make walls. They also wanted faster and cheaper ways of connecting the beams to the columns. Rivets replaced bolts, and then, in the late 1960s, a new style of construction emerged that could have deadly consequences.

Instead of bolts and rivets, steel columns and beams were welded together in a new process called flux-cored arc welding. The new method used rolled-up coiled wire instead of single sticks of welding metal, so the joints between columns and beams could be welded at the building site rather than manufactured elsewhere. A study in the early 1970s concluded that this method of welding beams to columns was stronger than bolting them together. "Engineers began using it ubiquitously," Hamburger says. "So not only did we think it was great, we said, 'You can't use anything else unless you prove yours is as good.'" A whole generation of US towers was built with welded steel joints. The problem became obvious in the 1994 Northridge earthquake: a long list of relatively new buildings suffered significant cracking in the welded steel. Then, a year to the day later, hundreds of steel-frame buildings were damaged in Japan's Kobe earthquake, and dozens of older ones collapsed.

Engineers have now known of the problem for more than a quarter century. But most of these buildings have not been strengthened, despite the fact that thousands of people still live and work inside them. Towers with welded joints between beams and columns can be made more resilient, but it's not easy and it's not cheap. The joints have to be exposed, which isn't just a simple case of cutting away drywall; fire-proofing material often has to be removed as well. And if the building predates 1979, it likely includes asbestos, which has to be treated as a hazardous material. Re-welding a joint or adding strengthening plates can cost up to $20,000 for a single joint. Hamburger estimates his office tower has approximately sixty joints on each of its thirty-three floors. It's easy to see how the cost of retrofitting a single building can quickly add up to tens of millions of dollars. Some owners have decided it's a cost worth paying, especially if they want to lease space to government agencies, which have higher minimum safety standards. But for now, many vulnerable welds remain.

Hamburger is quick to say he believes most towers will not collapse. Only a small fraction of them, he says, will experience the strongest ground-shaking possible. Still, the implications of even one collapse are terrifying, and Hamburger knows this better than most. He was a member of the building-performance assessment team that investigated the World Trade Center collapse in New York. He has a souvenir of his work: a large, mangled bolt he found at Ground Zero: a reminder that even giant modern towers can come crashing down.

It's impossible to walk through the deep-shadowed canyons of San Francisco's downtown streets and not wonder about the welded-steel skyscrapers. What will happen to them when a quake strikes that is comparable to the one in 1906? How many will be strengthened before then? Despite its many advances, California, too, is living on borrowed time.

TWO The Middle

Chapter 6
THE BIG ONE COMING TO THE BEEHIVE STATE

There hasn't been much shaking in Utah from a seismic standpoint since Brigham Young and 147 Mormon settlers rolled into the Salt Lake Valley in 1847. The long trek west started the previous year in Illinois—where an angry mob killed the religion's founder, Joseph Smith—and was motivated by a strong desire to escape the more violent aspects of life.

"This is the right place," Young declared as he and his entourage set up camp in the stark, arid landscape. At the time, Mexico claimed the sparsely populated outpost, but it would eventually become the capital of the forty-fifth state in the union. Other settlers and Indigenous groups had come through in the past, but most had moved on quickly, choosing to leave the dry ground and salt water in search of fertile ground and fresh water. But Young and other Mormon apostles decided the nearby streams, open space, and quiet would make it the perfect place to practice their religion in peace. Thousands of Latter-day Saints soon followed, and Utah became a "New Zion" for Mormons. For many of the faithful, it's been a peaceful place ever since. But the geological record tells a more turbulent story.

Hundreds of times each year, small earthquakes of magnitude 3 or lower shake Utah. It also experiences moderate shakers every few decades. But much bigger seismic events occurred in the past, and geologists say those past quakes are a clear indication of what is to come. As the old saying goes, it's a question of when, not if. When the next big earthquake shakes Utah, it will likely happen along the Wasatch fault, a 390-kilometre-long series of faults that hug the western slopes of the Wasatch Mountains, which in turn form the western edge of the Rockies. The Wasatch Fault Zone can cause earthquakes as large as magnitude 7.5. This is a particular concern because roughly 80 percent of Utah's three million residents live within twenty-five kilometres of the Wasatch Fault Zone.

Geologists have been aware of this seismic hotspot for a long time and have studied it thoroughly since the 1980s. The US Geological Survey and the Utah Geological Survey have measured and mapped all of the zone that shows evidence of surface-faulting during the Holocene epoch, or the last 11,700 years, and found ample evidence of large earthquakes of magnitude 6.5 or greater. A lot of that evidence is apparent right on the surface in the form of long, jagged, scar-like fault lines. When earthquakes of magnitude 6.5 or greater rumble deep down in the Earth's crust, they produce enough vertical movement to crack the surface. These cracks rip lines called scarps along the ground. These abrupt vertical walls are often several metres high and are the unmistakable footprints of past earthquakes. Over the past six thousand years, these relatively large earthquakes have occurred somewhere along the Wasatch every two hundred to three hundred years. And since no earthquakes of this size are known to have occurred in the area since 1847, geologists say the odds of one striking in the next half-century are high.

In 2010 the USGS and the UGS established the Working Group on Utah Earthquake Possibilities to estimate the odds of a magnitude-6.75 or greater quake hitting the state in the next fifty years. The answer was a headline-grabbing 43 percent, odds that surprised even the seismologist who chaired the working group.

"We were actually shocked the number was as high as it was," Ivan Wong said. Geologists have also homed in on the risk facing Salt Lake City specifically. That segment of the Wasatch fault ruptures every 1,300 to 1,500 years on average, and the evidence shows the last time it did so was 1,400 years ago. A report prepared for the Utah Seismic Safety Commission in 2015 compared the situation to Russian roulette: "the Wasatch fault beneath the Salt Lake Valley is 'loaded,' but we don't know whether the next Big One will strike soon or many decades from now."

When it does strike, it will cause several different types of destruction. Many old brick buildings in Salt Lake City and Utah's smaller towns are extremely vulnerable. A 2015 study tallied almost 150,000 unreinforced masonry buildings in Utah's twelve most northern counties. That represents only about 20 percent of all of the structures in that area, but it comprises a much higher proportion of the anticipated problems. Ninety thousand of those masonry buildings would suffer moderate damage or total destruction in a magnitude-7 quake. Many more would be damaged or destroyed in the powerful aftershocks that are likely to follow. Local politicians have made some small efforts to try to address this. Salt Lake City now offers a modest Fix the Bricks grant for homeowners, but the money is limited, and the list of people who want to take part is long. Without a major increase in the program's budget, it will take decades to fix all of the city's vulnerable buildings.

The 2015 study forecasts thousands of deaths and injuries if those vulnerable brick buildings aren't strengthened before the earth shakes. Many are single-family homes, but a lot of schools and hospitals are on the list as well. A vulnerable hospital is, of course, a double risk. Not only could patients and medical staff be hurt or killed in a collapse, but the community would also lose critical and desperately needed resources. Fifteen of the thirty-two hospital buildings studied would suffer at least moderate damage, putting more than 1,500 of 4,790 hospital beds out of commission.

But the risk of brick buildings falling down isn't Utah's only concern. A serious tremor will precipitate serious flooding, a real threat in the quickly growing suburbs northwest of Salt Lake City, where subsidence could cause the ground to settle at a lower elevation than it was before the quake. That, in turn, could cause lake water to break through flood-control dikes, flooding oil refineries, a sewage plant, and a growing area of residential and commercial development. Rising floodwaters could even reach Salt Lake City International Airport and Interstate 15. Several other highways will likely close if some of the many bridges they cross are damaged. Where bridges collapse, they will close both the highways they support and any roads or other infrastructure below. And while many of the freeway bridges in Utah have been built or upgraded since modern seismic standards were adopted, and are therefore unlikely to collapse completely, road displacement of only a few inches can make a bridge impassable.

Liquefaction is also a huge concern, especially in the low-lying ground near Great Salt Lake and Jordan River where the shaking would loosen up silt, sand, and gravel. If the water already mixed in with that sediment is shaken up and can't escape, it will cause once-solid ground to dissolve into a viscous, liquid-like state. Within seconds, buildings and other big structures that once stood on seemingly solid ground would have little or no support. In some cases, lateral spreading could literally rip open the soil underneath buildings, which in turn would split floors and walls. Other buildings could simply tip over as the soil below loses its rigid nature and can no longer support the weight. Liquefaction also forces buried holding tanks to float up to the surface and creates miniature sand volcanoes. These spontaneous outbursts can crack pipelines, causing dangerous leaks that often lead to fires and explosions. Sewer pipes can lose their downward slope and spread contaminated water and disease.

Liquefaction can cause as much (or more) damage as the shaking itself. It was a major destructive and costly factor in the devastating earthquake that shook Kobe, Japan, in 1995. Certainly the deaths of more than six thousand people constituted tremendous loss, but the city also suffered crippling economic injuries that lingered for years. Almost all of the electricity, gas, and water supplies were destroyed in the quake's immediate aftermath. And Kobe's port facilities were decimated, the main roads to the harbour cut off and almost all of the wharves left inoperable. Roughly twenty seconds of violent shaking and the liquefaction that followed flattened one of the world's busiest ports. Another illustrative, if frightening, example of liquefaction occurred in the 1964 Alaska earthquake, in the Anchorage neighbourhood of Turnagain Heights. The damp, silty soil was strong enough to support houses and other buildings as long as the ground stood still, but intense shaking rapidly transformed the soil from a solid to a liquid. Seventy-five homes sunk into the liquefied soil, which promptly slid into the ocean.

Even when the soil doesn't liquefy, big earthquakes can cause massive landslides. And in a mountainous state like Utah, that amounts to a serious threat to public safety. Co-seismic landslides, as they're known to scientists, occur when an earthquake shakes a mountainous area. One strong quake can cause hundreds or even thousands of landslides, and some of those slides can be deadly. If a magnitude-7 shakes Utah, geologists predict hundreds of landslides composed of soil and rock. Many will thunder down mountain slopes in remote parts of the state where few people, if any, reside. But deadly landslides are also possible in urban areas, including the suburbs of Salt Lake City.

Steep Mountain is a ridge that looms above a modern residential development in the Salt Lake Valley, about a half-hour drive south of downtown Salt Lake City. At its peak, it reaches 1,884 metres above sea level. Steep Mountain Drive, lined with single-family homes, winds its way along the southeast edge of this pleasant suburb. The homes on the north side of the road back onto other homes and parks; the homes on the south side stand in the shadow of Steep Mountain, its scrubby slope rising up at a relatively steady sixty-five to sixty-seven degrees. Researchers identified Steep Mountain as a risk of producing earthquake-induced landslides in 1987, but many houses have been built in the shadow of the mountain since then. A 2008 study for the Utah Geological Survey concluded the building setbacks are inadequate to protect the houses.

Recent studies suggest that thirty-two thousand people were killed as a direct result of landslides when an earthquake caused horrific damage across the Loess Plateau in northern China in 1920. The magnitude-8.3 quake triggered 675 major landslides. Estimates of the total deaths vary widely from seventy-three thousand to more than three hundred thousand. Recent studies have concluded that a majority of victims were killed in houses that collapsed because of the shaking. Many others succumbed to the bitter December cold. The hills in the region are made mostly of loess, a brittle yellow sediment of sand, silt, and clay that grows thicker, not stronger, with the accumulation of wind-blown dust. The loess slopes were several hundred metres deep in some locations and especially prone to sliding.

Half a century later, in 1970, a very different type of co-seismic landslide proved deadly in Peru. The giant earthquake that triggered it rumbled out of the sea floor under the Pacific and destabilized the north wall of Mount Huascarán, a colossal snow-capped peak that rises more than 6,700 metres above sea level. The size of the 1970 slide was enormous: a mass of rock and ice more than nine hundred metres wide and 1.6 kilometres long plummeted down the steep, slippery glacial slope at speeds of three hundred, possibly even four hundred, kilometres an hour. It plowed down towards the town of Yungay and surrounding villages, picking up rocks, mud, trees, and everything else in its path as it went. It swelled in size to an estimated one hundred million cubic metres and enveloped Yungay less than two minutes after the earthquake sent thousands of frightened people into the streets. The mass of mud washed over a two-hundred-metre-high hill and buried almost everyone in Yungay within seconds. Only a few outcrops of high ground escaped the deadly deluge, one of which supported a large, white statue of Jesus, his arms stretched over the destruction below.

Peruvian officials never determined exactly how many people died, because so many bodies could not be recovered. Even estimates were difficult because the tragedy took place on a market day, when people flocked into town, but some suggest as many as twenty-two thousand people died in Yungay and the surrounding villages. The survivors numbered only in the hundreds, the largest group a collection of about three hundred children who'd gathered in a circus tent. The clown who'd been entertaining them acted decisively and shepherded all three hundred uphill to safety as soon as the shaking stopped, "like the Pied Piper," according to one of the few surviving adults.

For all the troubling questions about how Utah will fare in a big earthquake, the state has worked in recent years to find geological answers in an attempt to better identify the natural hazard. The bad news, according to the experts, is that the response to that hazard has been inadequate. In 2016 seismologist Ivan Wong delivered a blunt message to the Utah Seismic Safety Commission: "The attitude that the 'big one' will not occur in one's lifetime and that the threat can be ignored must change." Wong identified a number of concerns and emphasized schools in particular. Without more preparations, the Earthquake Engineering Institute's Utah chapter predicts as many as 2,500 deaths in the state, and thousands more injuries, in a magnitude-7 earthquake along the Wasatch fault. More than fifty thousand would need shelter, and the financial cost could top $30 billion. The overwhelming majority would survive, but the disruption to the lives of survivors would be profound.

The losses could be significantly reduced if the people, businesses, and governments of Utah do more to prepare. Some of those preparations have started. Driving north along Interstate 15 towards downtown Salt Lake City, it's hard not to be inspired by the mix of modern and historic buildings, framed by the impressive Wasatch Mountains. If you park near the Mormon Tabernacle, you can walk through Temple Square, a ten-acre complex that is the headquarters of the Church of Jesus Christ of Latter-day Saints. Temple Square offers a glimpse of the Utah State Capitol, a neoclassical building perched on a massive plinth that sits atop a hill. The Capitol looms above the city like one of the Roman temples that inspired its design. In a city built around the church, the Capitol is an unmistakable reminder of the earthly power of government. The exterior walls are made of Utah granite and guarded by a wide rank of perfectly spaced Corinthian columns. At the top is a magnificent copper-clad concrete dome that weighs around thirty million pounds. In the Capitol's halls, marble rosettes and Roman arches mingle with sculptures and paintings. Large murals depict the history and culture of this unique state, from Mormon colonization to the history of agriculture. It's not surprising that many people in the state want to see the Capitol preserved.

State legislators first learned in the 1990s that the Capitol could collapse in a major earthquake. The imposing structure was built of concrete, granite, and marble. Though some reinforcing steel was used in the concrete, it was minimal by modern standards. Engineers warned lawmakers that the weight above and around them could come crashing down. But what could be done about it? Strengthening the Capitol and preserving the building's art and architecture would be a complex, expensive undertaking. After considering a number of options, the state settled on a seismic retrofit plan that was as big and expensive as it was unusual. Engineers designed a base-isolation system that included more than 250 shock-absorbers underneath the building that would allow it to move as much as sixty centimetres in any direction. Those shock-absorbers would be made of rubber and steel and would be placed under the building's foundation, after much of that foundation was replaced. In 2004 legislative staff moved out while construction crews got started with the painstaking work in the basement. After injecting grout into the soil under the footings, they went to work cutting into the concrete. They could jack up portions of the building no more than one-sixteenth of an inch. The existing columns were cut at the base and the foundation beneath replaced with new foundations and base isolators.

The four giant footings that supported the dome presented an especially daunting challenge. The weight was enormous, so engineers decided not to excavate under those footings. Instead, they built large concrete beams that wrapped around the existing footings and rested on top of long steel girders, which in turn rested on dozens of steel and rubber base-isolation pads. The end result was that the massive dome and the rest of the building were isolated from the ground. They should be able to remain relatively stable while the rest of Salt Lake City rocks back and forth.

Base isolation is still relatively rare, but the Utah Capitol is far from the only example of it. The Salt Lake City and County Building was also strengthened with base isolators, as were city halls in Los Angeles, San Francisco, and other California cities. Engineers say it's a good method for strengthening historic buildings, but it has also been used on modern buildings like the eight-storey AutoZone headquarters in downtown Memphis. The Mormon Church also turned to the technology, announcing in 2019 that the Salt Lake Temple would be closed for a seismic retrofit that included hundreds of base isolators installed under its foundations. Church leaders hoped the giant shock-absorbers would preserve one of their most cherished spaces, which the president of the Church of Jesus Christ of Latter-day Saints called a "stunning jewel in the crown of pioneer achievement."

Not long after the seismic work started, the Salt Lake Temple received a surprise test run when the ground under the Utah capital started shaking on March 18, 2020. It measured as magnitude 5.7, and the Utah Division of Emergency Management said it was the strongest quake to shake the region since 1992. The temblor damaged dozens of brick buildings and some mobile homes in and around Salt Lake City, thirty-one thousand litres of hydrochloric acid leaked from a tank at a copper refinery, a radio station lost its transmitter tower, and at least two schools suffered serious damage. At the top of the temple's sixty-four-metre central spire, a golden trumpet was dislodged from the grip of the Angel Moroni statue. To the faithful, the angel's horn symbolizes their duty to share their faith with others. For scientists working in Utah, the seismic event that shook the horn free was a reminder that a much bigger quake is on the way—and of the opportunity to prepare before it comes.

Divya Chandrasekhar was at home with her three-year-old son that March day. Though she studies disaster planning for a living, the University of Utah professor needed a moment to realize exactly what was going on. The last earthquake she'd lived through was more than twenty years earlier in New Delhi. As soon as she knew it was an earthquake, she dropped, covered her son, and held on. When the shaking stopped she and her son left the house quickly so they wouldn't be caught inside during an aftershock, even though the engineer who'd inspected her wood-frame house before she'd moved in had deemed it unlikely to collapse. Almost all the other houses in her neighbourhood were made of brick, and yet Chandrasekhar didn't see anyone else seeking safety outside. That's not to say people weren't frightened; far from it. The earthquake made headlines and led all the local newscasts because people were scared stiff and buildings suffered serious damage. But a lot of people in Salt Lake City simply didn't know what to do when the earthquake struck. That's not necessarily surprising in Utah, where frightening earthquakes are a rarity. Millions of Californians may have memories of the ground shaking, but for most people in Utah in early 2020, an earthquake was a mostly hypothetical scenario. While the shaking may have shown how unprepared many people and buildings were, it was also a gift of sorts, because it was scary enough for people to take notice and start thinking about preparation. "This was the disaster of our dreams," Chandrasekhar enthused. "When children die, it makes the most amount of news, but we don't want children to die."

Like many experts in disaster planning, Chandrasekhar's dream is that Utah will get ready now, before a really big earthquake strikes. While other experts and engineers have conducted important research into building design and resilience, Chandrasekhar has focused on how to make people resilient. She's conducted extensive research into how communities, households, and individuals recover from disasters and looked specifically at New York after Hurricane Sandy, Puerto Rico after Hurricane Maria, New Orleans after Hurricane Katrina, and Banda Aceh after the 2004 earthquake and tsunami. Time and again, she says, a community's ability to respond to disaster reflects how well it has prepared: "Of course what happens after the disaster is so much related to what happened before the disaster." But deciding you need to do more to prepare is one thing, and knowing what specifically needs to be done is another.

Although Utah is woefully unprepared in some areas, like the seismic retrofit of old buildings, Chandrasekhar believes the state should focus on two priorities immediately. First, she thinks the state should build more affordable housing. She acknowledges mandatory retrofits of old brick buildings, like the regulations California has adopted, can save lives. But they can also take decades to achieve results, and Chandrasekhar believes building affordable new housing can be a faster way to make people safe than leaving them waiting inside vulnerable old buildings. Her second priority is to develop more support for small businesses and help them better prepare for an earthquake or other disaster. This may not seem an obvious priority for emergency preparedness, but Chandrasekhar sees small businesses as both economic lifelines and de facto social service agencies in many communities, providing jobs and in-person social networks that can prove crucial when a community is trying to recover from a disaster. In Utah, however, the social function of small business may be less crucial than in many other jurisdictions because of what Chandrasekhar considers one of the state's biggest assets in terms of resilience: the Mormon religion. Sixty-two percent of the state's 3.2 million residents were Mormon in 2018, and having such a large segment of the population share so many values has some benefits. Chandrasekhar considers the religion's "ethos of self-resilience" a real strength that might mean many more people are prepared when the earth finally shakes.

The March 2020 quake shook Utah just as people were starting to stay home and self-isolate because of the Coronavirus pandemic. Like so many other places around the world, the state suffered terrible economic losses from the pandemic, and small businesses were hit especially hard. While many Utah businesses suffered a double loss from the earthquake and the COVID-19 shutdown, Chandrasekhar hopes the events of 2020 might turn out to be a double blessing for the state in the long run.

Chapter 7
SHAKING DOWN THE MISSISSIPPI

On a cold winter night in 1811, nine days before Christmas, the soft soils on the banks of the mighty Mississippi River started to shudder. In the little frontier town of New Madrid, roughly four hundred people were jolted out of their beds as the ground under them heaved and rolled. The Spanish had first welcomed American settlers to this remote outpost across the river from Kentucky in the 1770s, then in 1800 they swapped the vast territory surrounding it with France for another piece of the colonial puzzle. The United States secured the sleepy settlement as part of the Louisiana Purchase in 1803 and in 1812 renamed the expanse west of New Madrid the Missouri Territory. But at 2 a.m. on December 16, 1811, the town's inhabitants were more concerned with tremors than territorial declarations.

Five years later, in a letter to a friend, New Madrid resident Eliza Bryan recalled that terrifying night. "We were visited by a violent shock of an earthquake," she wrote, "accompanied by a very awful noise resembling loud but distant thunder, but more hoarse and vibrating." A few minutes after the shaking stopped, Bryan experienced "a complete saturation of the atmosphere, with sulphurious vapor, causing total darkness. The screams of the affrighted inhabitants running to and fro, not knowing where to go, or what to do—the cries of the fowls and beasts of every species—the cracking of trees falling, and the roaring of the Mississippi—the current of which was retrograde for a few minutes, owing as is supposed, to an irruption in its bed—formed a scene truly horrible."

Other witnesses saw thick, fully grown cottonwood trees snap in half. Some townsfolk described the ground rolling in waves, as if it were made of water, while the real water of the Mississippi River raged wildly in all directions. Many cabins and houses sunk deep into the mud, some submerged completely. Hunters brought back tales of the earth ripping open and countless geysers spraying mud, sand, and even coal skywards. Once-fertile soil was covered in white sand and looked like a beach. Other land was submerged, leaving farmers to wade for miles through muddy water. Several large landslides occurred as well, from where Memphis now stands all the way up to southern Illinois.

In St. Louis, 240 kilometres upstream from New Madrid, the quake caused panic. "I was roused from my sleep by the clamor of windows, doors, furniture in tremulous motion, with a distant rumbling noise resembling a number of carriages passing over pavement," editor Joseph Charless wrote in the *Louisiana Gazette*, St. Louis's first newspaper. Strong tremors rumbled intermittently for the next few hours, and when the sun came up, Charless said, the sky was hazy and the air unusually warm for the season. "The houses and fences appeared covered with a white frost, but on examination it was found to be vapour, not possessing the chilling cold of frost: indeed the moon was enshrouded in awful gloom."

Though startling, the big shock on December 16 was just the start of three months of terrifying shaking in the region that included countless aftershocks and a total of three separate quakes. People in Nashville counted more than fifty frightening tremors in the three weeks following the first shock. Up and down the valley, hundreds of aftershocks came and went. Many were left to wonder if the world was coming to an end, as this passenger on board a southbound river boat confided in a letter to a friend: "From the long continuance and frequency of these shocks, it is extremely uncertain when they will cease; and if they have been as heavy at New Orleans as we have felt them, the consequences must be dreadful indeed; and I am fearful when I arrive at Natchez to hear that the whole city of Orleans is entirely demolished, and perhaps sunk."

The aftershocks continued into the new year before another major earthquake occurred on January 23. The seismic unrest kept many people in an almost constant state of terror and, according to one Catholic priest writing to his bishop in faraway Quebec, "helped much to bring people back to their religion."

On February 7 the final, and possibly biggest, of the seismic triple bill played out when another gigantic tremor rocked the region and nearly destroyed New Madrid. "The town of New Madrid has sunk 12 feet below its former standing," the *Alexandria Daily Gazette* reported. "The houses are all thrown down, and the inhabitants moved off, except the French, who live in camps close to the river side, and have their boats tied near them in order to sail off, in case the earth should sink." But not all boats were safe. The paper reported one sank with a family inside. And even on boats that didn't sink, some people had reason to fear for their safety as the river water beneath them appeared to bubble and boil. Those who weren't killed in the earthquake itself were left to wander in chaos. "No pencil can paint the distresses of the many movers!" the *Daily Gazette* wrote. "Men, women, and children, barefooted and naked! Without money and without food!"

In some instances the shaking was so strong that the Mississippi River itself was thrown around like water in a bathtub. Many witnesses believed they saw stretches of the river flow backwards for short spells as certain segments of land heaved higher than the upstream portions of riverbed. Riverboat crews twenty-seven kilometres south of New Madrid claimed the water level rapidly rose six feet, and the water flowed three times faster than it had the night before. Flat-bottom boats lying along the shore were destroyed. The first steamboat on the Mississippi, *The New Orleans*, on her maiden voyage at the time, was moored to an island before one of the quakes, only to find that island sinking beneath the surface a few hours later. In other stretches, the river burst its banks, bubbled into rapids, and swallowed thousands of trees. In *Travels in the Interior of America*, John Bradbury described seeing "the river agitated as if by a storm…I could distinctly hear the crash of falling trees, and the screaming of wild fowl on the river." He also described the sound of the event, as "the most violent tempest of wind mixed with a sound equal to the loudest thunder, but more hollow and vibrating." Another man, who had been on a large barge a few miles downstream from New Madrid, told the *Knoxville Gazette* that "the river rose several feet; the trees on the shore shook; the banks in the large columns tumbled in; hundreds of old trees that had lain perhaps half a century at the bottom of the river, appeared on the surface of the water."

There was no official death toll in the sparsely populated territory, but people were indeed killed, some drowned in surging river waters, others crushed in collapsing cabins and barns. "We lost our Amandy Jane in this one," George Heinrich Crist wrote in Nelson, Kentucky. "A log fell on her. We will bury her upon the hill under a clump of trees where Besys Ma and Pa is buried. A lot of people think that the devil has come here. Some thinks that this is the beginning of the world coming to an end." Like many who had lived through the tremors, Crist struggled to make sense of what had occurred. "What are we gonna do? You cannot fight it cause you do not know how. It is not something that you can see. In a storm you can see the sky and it shows dark clouds and you know that you might get strong winds but this you can not see anything but a house that just lays in a pile on the ground—not scattered around and trees that just falls over with the roots still on it." Crist wanted to leave, but like many of his neighbours, he complained that, months later, he still could not find or buy enough animals to pull his wagons.

Eventually the suffering prompted a significant intervention from the federal government. In 1814, two years after the final quake, the Missouri Territory governor, William Clark—of the famous Lewis and Clark Expedition, ten years earlier—requested financial aid from Washington for the people of New Madrid County. Congress sent $50,000 the following year; it was the first time Congress sent money to a region hit by a natural disaster.

At the time, there was little doubt that these earthquakes were calamitous events, and that the victims needed help. Since then, however, some have expressed doubt. Seismic measuring equipment that could provide accurate readings of magnitude did not exist, but scientists study historical reports that describe the intensity of shaking in various locations, and couple it with what they know about the faults in the area, to estimate the magnitude of historical earthquakes. Several geologists estimate the three New Madrid quakes were in the mid-7s. The third may have been as large as magnitude 8. Others, however, argue the New Madrid Seismic Zone could never produce a magnitude 8 and that the temblors in 1811 and 1812 must have been closer to magnitude 7. That's an important difference, as a magnitude-8 event is ten times bigger than a magnitude-7 event and releases thirty-one times as much energy. A magnitude-7 quake is much smaller than a magnitude-8, but it is still a gigantic event, and it would be catastrophic if one were to happen today.

The New Madrid Seismic Zone now includes major cities like Memphis and St. Louis, and the threat has increased as the population has grown. A major quake in the Mississippi River valley and farther afield is a concern because seismic waves in this region tend to travel so much farther than they do on the West Coast. The rock under the fertile soils of the Mississippi River valley is composed largely of sedimentary rock—like shale, sandstone, and limestone — that doesn't suppress seismic waves as much as the granite that's common along the West Coast. While the magnitude-7.9 1906 San Francisco earthquake was felt more than five hundred kilometres away in Nevada, the 1811 earthquake in Missouri was felt nearly 1,600 kilometres away and may have affected an area roughly ten times as large as the San Francisco quake.

The New Madrid Seismic Zone has a long reach, and the central Mississippi River valley is the source of more earthquakes than anywhere else in the United States east of the Rocky Mountains. In 2008, the Federal Emergency Management Agency warned of "widespread and catastrophic damage across eight states that are home to 44 million people," if a quake similar to the 1811 one happened today. An agency spokesperson warned the people who live and build in the valley to prepare for the "catastrophic earthquake" that is expected.

Although no one can say when the next big earthquake will hit the region, scientists warn it could happen while many of us are still alive. The US Geological Survey estimates the risk of it happening in the next fifty years at roughly 10 percent. It's between 25 and 40 percent likely that a smaller though still deadly magnitude-6 earthquake will occur during that time.

The New Madrid Seismic Zone stretches far and wide over the fertile fields of the Mississippi River valley. The area extends across portions of seven or eight states, and contains one of the world's largest liquefaction zones. A 2009 study estimated a magnitude-7.7 quake in the region would cause serious damage to more than 3,500 bridges. More than 2.5 million households would be left with no electricity, and more than one million with no water. Seven hundred thousand buildings would be damaged, 80,000 people would be injured, and 3,500 would be killed. The projected economic toll is a staggering $300 billion. And yet none of the vulnerable states or municipalities compel building owners to perform seismic retrofits. Jim Wilkinson, the executive director of the Central United

States Earthquake Consortium, calls it a tough sell. For the most part, he says, residents of these states don't associate earthquakes with where they live. "You say earthquake, and people just think California."

That attitude stems from the absence of a big earthquake in living memory and the fact that other natural hazards are more common. Tornado warning signs abound, because the United States gets more violent tornadoes than any other country. While tornadoes can occur almost anywhere, they're much more prone to happen between 30° and 50° latitude, where colder polar air collides with warmer subtropical air and creates strong thunderstorms. Most tornadoes in the United States happen in the Midwest and the South. The worst ones, like the Tri-State Tornado in 1925, can kill hundreds of people and injure thousands. More than a thousand tornadoes touch down every year in America, according to the National Oceanic and Atmospheric Administration.

Floods also lurk in the minds of Midwesterners. The Mississippi River and its tributaries drain thirty-two states and two Canadian provinces, carrying thousands of cubic metres of water per second down to the Gulf of Mexico. Hurricanes and heavy rains have overwhelmed the great river on several occasions. In the spring of 1927, floods affected Illinois, Indiana, Missouri, Kentucky, Texas, Oklahoma, Kansas, Tennessee, Arkansas, Mississippi, and Louisiana. Near the city of Vicksburg in western Mississippi, the river swelled to more than 120 kilometres wide. When the high water finally receded, months later, hundreds were dead and more than seven hundred thousand were left homeless. The flood cost roughly $1 billion, one-third of the federal budget at the time. In the years that followed, governments invested in flood-control measures, although nothing can eliminate the risk entirely.

It's understandable that people up and down the Mississippi River would be more preoccupied with both floods and tornadoes, but the risk of damaging earthquakes remains significant. The next big event may be three hundred years away, or it could happen tomorrow. "It doesn't have to be the historical mid-seven kind of event," Wilkinson notes. A quake in the low sixes is much more likely to happen, he says, and it could be devastating. "But again, it is a tough sell. Folks just don't want to be forced or told what to do. We have a constant challenge with building code adoption, because there are groups out there that will say that everything that we're talking about is made up or inflated, and essentially we're just trying to keep our jobs by talking about earthquakes." Wilkinson has been trying to sell several states and cities on some basic seismic precautions, like tougher retrofit requirements for old brick buildings. But that costs money, and he knows from years of trying that people are reluctant to spend money to guard against something they have never experienced.

The skepticism is also the result of an earthquake that wasn't, a memorable affair that happened (or didn't) in New Madrid in 1990. The town had grown to about three thousand but was still a relatively sleepy place. But there was a big-city buzz in New Madrid when the sun crept up over the Mississippi River on the morning of Monday, December 3, because of a high-profile prediction that another big earthquake could strike the region that day. News crews from more than two hundred organizations, and at least thirty satellite trucks, had rolled into town over the weekend. Nervous school officials cancelled classes in New Madrid and parts of five surrounding states. The local chamber of commerce sold commemorative T-shirts for $12 (sweatshirts for $20), local restaurants added earthquake-themed menu items, and a nearby McDonald's offered free coffee—a "price you can shake and rattle about." The sign outside the First Baptist Church proclaimed: "GIVE PRAISE TO OUR GOD WHO CAN SHAKE THE EARTH IF HE WANTS TO." The Kewanee Missionary Baptist Church took a more subtle approach, offering "Eternity Preparedness Kits."

The bizarre scene was the result of a business consultant named Iben Browning and his oddly specific prognostication that a major earthquake in the region could occur on December 3. He had mentioned the date as early as 1985 in public lectures and had pegged the odds at 50 percent. Browning was a seventy-two-year-old from Albuquerque, New Mexico, who called himself a climatologist; he had earned a PhD in zoology many years earlier. He'd worked as a weapons systems analyst for the Sandia National Laboratories in New Mexico and as a NASA consultant before the 1969 moon landing. In the 1970s he wrote a number of books on subjects as varied as robotics and climatology and started publishing a newsletter that featured his climate predictions. Browning argued the world was entering an era of global cooling and scoffed at the greenhouse effect. He gained a following in the business community, especially from people with a financial stake in agricultural futures.

In late 1989, the *Memphis Commercial Appeal* reported Browning's prediction and described him as a "scientist who correctly predicted October's San Francisco earthquake." For his part, Browning insisted he did not release his prediction to the public and worried that "panic can kill more people than an earthquake." Still, media coverage of his attention-grabbing prediction picked up steam. Most scientists discounted the possibility, but many chose not to discuss it openly out of fear that doing so would only feed the publicity flames. Several reporters were skeptical about Browning's claims and couldn't make sense of his model for prediction, which seemed to rest largely on climate data. Some of those reporters spoke to seismologists who were astonished that anyone would take the prediction seriously. But then David Stewart, the director of Earthquake Studies at Southeast Missouri University, wrote a memo to colleagues calling Browning "perhaps, the most intelligent person I have ever met." Stewart didn't share the same opinion about the likelihood of an earthquake on any given day, but he argued Browning should be taken seriously. "Here's a man who verifiably has hit several home runs, and he's up to bat," he told the *Dallas Morning News.* "You can't ignore the batting record."

But had Iben Browning really hit home runs? The US Geological Survey was now taking the prediction more seriously—at least, it was taking the growing public concern more seriously—and assembled a panel of eleven seismic experts to look into Browning's claims. Seismologist Walt Hays arrived at a blunt conclusion: "Iben Browning's record for predicting earthquakes is about as good as that of someone throwing darts at a calendar." Hays said Browning had made only vague predictions. For instance, ten days before the 1989 Loma Prieta quake, Browning predicted several earthquakes would rumble around the world on October 16, a day before the actual event, but he didn't specify that any would happen in California. Similarly, six days before Mount St. Helens finally blew its top, he predicted it would erupt in the next week. Scientists were already closely monitoring the smoking mountain.

As summer turned into fall, however, public anxiety continued to rise. Then on September 26 a moderate tremor rocked the region and rattled nerves. By November, nervous residents could focus their seismic anxiety on an NBC miniseries, *The Big One: The Great Los Angeles Earthquake,* a fictional story with a strangely familiar plotline about a controversial earthquake prediction that came true. By the time the big day arrived in New Madrid, anticipation was at a fever pitch. Some were terrified; others openly mocked the idea that something so random as an earthquake could be predicted. December 3 came and went without a rumble, and a few months later, the National Anxiety Center awarded Iben Browning its first Chicken Little Award for scaring "the daylights out of people in seven Midwestern states," providing "one of the most dubious news stories of the year, and demonstrating the way anyone with a Ph.D. is given free rein to create a high level of public anxiety." The following summer, Browning died of a heart attack.

Life in those seven states gradually returned to normal, and most people who live in the Mississippi River valley went back to ignoring earthquakes. The hysteria arguably did as much harm to seismic-readiness efforts in the region as the lack of recent strong earthquakes. And while it's tempting to chalk the whole affair up to one misguided individual and his countless ignorant followers, it's important to note that Iben Browning wasn't the first person to try to predict an earthquake.

Chapter 8

THE PROBLEM WITH PREDICTION

Can earthquakes be predicted? No. That's the simple answer. And yet the dramatic story of an earthquake that was foretold in China, saving thousands of lives and convincing millions of people it might be possible to forecast future quakes in the way we now forecast storms, is worth recounting before we dismiss entirely the possibility of prediction.

In February 1975, a week before the Chinese New Year, a delegation of Communist Party officials from Anshan City visited the town of Dashiqiao, "to express good wishes and give a stage performance to entertain the Headquarters of the 39th Army." The formal ceremony and performance were standard fare in China at the time, but nothing about this time and place was typical. Dashiqiao was home to an earthquake office, established a few months earlier amid a flurry of strange natural phenomena. The head of the earthquake office was a local legend named Cao Xianqing, who was better known in Yingkou County as "Mr. Earthquake." Cao was not a scientist but a former soldier who had served with the People's Liberation Army in both the Chinese Civil War and the Korean War. He approached earthquake preparation with a fanaticism born of China's Cultural Revolution, which was winding down after a decade of political persecutions and ideological purges that killed at least four hundred thousand people and perhaps as many as ten million. In the last months of 1974, Cao stirred up considerable concern among locals, sometimes even causing widespread panic, with his talk of earthquakes, but on February 4 his fervour finally paid off, and it did so in dramatic fashion.

Shortly before 8 a.m. a magnitude-5.1 earthquake rattled the ground under Dashiqiao. Cao immediately convened a meeting of the Yingkou Party Committee at which he proclaimed that "a large earthquake may occur today during the day or evening." As a result, all business and production work was suspended, and most meetings and public activities were cancelled. The edict led to the cancellation of the stage performance that was scheduled for the Headquarters of the 39th Army that evening, but nervous local leaders refused to cancel the welcome ceremony for the cadre of party officials from Anshan City.

At the appointed time of 7 p.m., one thousand people gathered to take part in the formalities. All seven of the doors to the hall were kept open in case a rapid exit was needed. On stage, the hosts and honoured guests exchanged greetings, and the first of the dignitaries exited the building at 7:20 p.m. Everyone else followed them out in an orderly manner, and not a minute too soon. At 7:26, moments after the last person left the hall, the ground started heaving back and forth, and the hall collapsed. Not one person in the hall was killed, although Chinese officials claimed one soldier was injured as he escorted the last person away from the collapsing building.

The earthquake was recorded as magnitude 7.3, and it devastated the town. Two-thirds of all the buildings in Dashiqiao were destroyed, but out of seventy-two thousand people in the town, only twenty-one were killed—at least according to official reports. Local officials had closed shops and sports fields ahead of time. They'd relocated hospital patients and emptied a great many other buildings. Officials at the observatory in nearby Shipengyu warned locals to stay outside, and a movie operator helped by projecting outdoor films. Large crowds braved the cold temperatures to watch the films and, as a result, avoided being trapped inside their homes when the buildings collapsed.

Many stories of survival from that earthquake were attributed to heroic Communist officials, although most have not been independently confirmed. In one particularly startling story, Chinese officials claimed that 95 percent of the 28,000 rooms in the Yinglou Commune in Haicheng County collapsed, but because the homes were evacuated beforehand, only forty-four people died.

Scientists from the United States, Canada, New Zealand, and other countries visited China in the years immediately after the quake, and others returned decades later to study newly declassified documents. These later studies established that more than 2,000 people died, primarily in towns where local officials did not proactively evacuate buildings: more than 1,300 died in the quake itself, hundreds more died in the fires that followed, and others succumbed to freezing, suffocation, or carbon monoxide poisoning. In addition, more than 24,000 people were injured. But the quake would undoubtedly have killed many more people if local residents had not been warned beforehand. The American delegation that visited China in 1976 estimated "casualties in excess of 100,000 would have ordinarily been anticipated" in the region. In 2004, Kelin Wang and a team from the Geological Survey of Canada investigated the quake and agreed with the basic premise, concluding that "measures taken by various levels of government on 4 February 1975 in the Yingkou-Haicheng area indeed saved thousands of lives."

Human preparations saved lives in this exceedingly rare case, but how did Chinese officials predict an earthquake ahead of time? And did they really predict the quake, or did they simply respond to a rare set of clues before the quake happened?

China has had countless earthquakes over the millennia, but this part of the country had been relatively quiet until a trio of strong earthquakes shattered the silence in the late 1960s. The quakes appeared to be on the move, migrating from the southwest to the northeast. "The epicentres of recent strong earthquakes in the Bohai Bay area show a tendency of northward migration," one Chinese scientist wrote in a secret government document in 1970. "Jianxing and Yingkou that are located on the Bohai Bay may fall into this area of strong earthquakes and suffer destruction." With strong encouragement from the popular premier Zhou Enlai, China rapidly stepped up earthquake monitoring in the early 1970s, and a series of national conferences on prediction soon followed. Many scientists were skeptical of the idea but reluctant to speak out. The Cultural Revolution had closed universities and colleges, and intellectuals were regularly humiliated, jailed, or killed for stepping outside Communist Party lines. Earthquake science was one of the rare academic pursuits that the Communists valued, rather than accusing it of circumventing the revolution's progress. Geologists and government officials set up observatories across the countryside and enlisted thousands of local farmers as amateur observers. Scientists measured the electric currents in the ground and air and monitored known faults for any movements. They watched well water for the presence of telltale gases like radon and assigned amateur observers to track water colour and levels, both of which sometimes changed wildly.

They also documented unusual animal behaviour. Snakes awoke from their slumber and slithered out of their dens into the freezing air, where they promptly froze to death. Mice stumbled out of their holes, oblivious to cats and other predators that promptly took advantage of their good fortune. Frogs and rats exhibited unusual behaviour and farm animals seemed out of sorts, although skeptical scientists noted these incidents represented only a tiny fraction of the animals in the area. It was bizarre, however, and people wondered about the cause. Were vibrations from the underground rumblings to blame for the unusual animal behaviour? Had the increased seismic activity released poisonous gas into their dens?

It made it all the easier for "Mr. Earthquake" and other proactive officials to convince people that a big earthquake was coming.

The most convincing factor, though, was likely the hundreds of foreshocks that had started rumbling the ground under Haicheng and Yingkou Counties a few years earlier and become more frequent in the months preceding the big event. While some were not big enough to be felt, many were. Officials, convinced a big earthquake was imminent, evacuated many buildings in false alarms in the months before the February 4 quake struck.

False alarms are one of the big problems with trying to predict earthquakes. Causing panic or at least anxiety is harmful in and of itself. It can also be counterproductive. Too many false alarms might make people doubt the warnings, as happened with some of the people who lived in Crescent City, California, in 1964, who ignored the tsunami warning sirens that followed the Great Alaska Earthquake. Indeed, many Chinese officials in the 1970s worried that issuing false alarms would do more harm than good. Scientists at one earthquake planning conference urged local officials to avoid "causing panic and disturbance to the masses, interrupting production and people's living." In some towns, local officials followed this advice, only to see falling buildings crush their community when the quake came to life and find themselves roundly criticized, especially when compared to the success of "Mr. Earthquake" and his precautions. But it might be argued that Cao and officials like him saved lives because they ignored the sensible advice of scientists. In essence, they had luck on their side. Kelin Wang concluded as much in 2006: "the prediction of the Haicheng earthquake was a blend of confusion, empirical analysis, intuitive judgement, and good luck."

At the time, however, most of China's eight hundred million people believed that scientists had finally cracked the earthquake code. Indeed, Communist officials encouraged this belief. "This is eloquent proof," the *Peking Review*, the party's English-language propaganda newspaper, boasted, "that in socialist New China, under the leadership of Chairman Mao and the Communist Party and by relying on the masses and professional seismological workers armed with Marxism-Leninism-Mao Tzetung thought and persevering in practice, forecasts can be made and damage can be greatly minimized by doing a good job of precautionary work." But one of the worst tragedies in recorded history would prove China's confidence in earthquake prediction false.

The Great Tangshan Earthquake struck a little less than five hundred kilometres to the southwest of the Haicheng earthquake in the summer of 1976. Some agencies registered it as a 7.6, others as 7.8. The quake was felt as far away as Mongolia in the west and Korea in the east. It caused considerable damage and fifty deaths in Beijing, about 180 kilometres west. But the damage in the capital paled in comparison to the suffering inflicted on the industrial city of Tangshan, where approximately one million people lived. The city is situated at the junction of several fault zones with a long history of seismic activity. (In fact, an active fault line ran right under the city, but scientists had not yet discovered it.) The Tangshan quake flattened it.

Most people in Tangshan lived in one- to three-storey brick houses or poorly built apartment towers. The designs for many of the brick houses dated back to nineteenth-century British mine owners. The typical house consisted of a heavy concrete roof, often scrap material, perched on top of unreinforced brick walls. The apartment towers followed Soviet designs, but many were poorly built under the supervision of inadequately trained Chinese architects. At the time of the quake, only a tiny fraction of the city's buildings had been designed with seismic safety in mind.

Nearly everyone in the city was asleep at 3:42 a.m. when the quake occurred. Its epicentre was shallow and tragically close to the city. The energy unleashed was the rough equivalent of four hundred atomic bombs. Anyone could easily confuse photographs of Tangshan with images of Hiroshima or Nagasaki. Ten thousand coal miners on the night shift emerged from their mines to find Tangshan in ruins. They'd been relatively safe underground, where shaking is typically less severe and the round shape of mine shafts helps them withstand pressure. Roughly 85 percent of the buildings had collapsed, and hundreds of thousands of people were dead. As the deafening roar of the quake and the collapse subsided, a chorus of cries and moans rose. People choked and coughed as a thick cloud of dust enveloped the city.

Tangshan was incapacitated, in the truest sense of the word. Stunned survivors stumbled to local hospitals in search of medical care but found only rubble and death. They found the same at police stations and government buildings. The central train station collapsed. But the airport, a one-level terminal built with Soviet support in the 1950s, remained standing. In the days following the quake, a steady stream of planes with emergency supplies landed. The demand was overwhelming. Doctors at the airport operated as if in a military field hospital, amputating limbs without anesthetics and leaving severely injured patients to die in order to focus on those who had a fighting chance.

The roads and railway lines into Tangshan were damaged and buckled beyond quick repair, so soldiers from the People's Liberation Army had to march in on foot. For many, the walk took them days, and when they arrived they found few supplies. Many, desperately thirsty, resorted to drinking contaminated water. They joined local survivors in working frantically to rescue thousands of trapped people, digging through the rubble with little more than their hands. Some lost their fingernails. More often than not, though, the fading cries for help fell silent before victims could be saved. Some died mere metres away from rescuers, on the other side of seemingly impenetrable brick and concrete. But several thousand people were saved. Zhang Zhiqin, a sales clerk, went to sleep that night inside the three-storey shop where she worked. She woke up with the building collapsing around her. "I will never forget the choking dust as the building collapsed," she told the *South China Morning Post* thirty years after the tragedy. "It was so dark I couldn't see my fingers." Zhang waited for hours before realizing that she would have to try to escape herself. She pulled herself through the rubble inch by inch. Finally, her hands felt a small hole, and she mustered enough voice to call for help. Soldiers were able to hear her, find her, and pull her to safety.

At least 240,000 people died in the Great Tangshan Earthquake. (That number is a count of the victims who had been permanent residents of Tangshan City and does not include the deaths of many villagers or people who had moved to Tangshan from other parts of China. The overall death toll was likely closer to half a million and possibly higher.) If the Haicheng earthquake looked like a major triumph for earthquake prediction, the Tangshan quake looked like a deadly failure. But neither characterization is entirely accurate. Officials in Haicheng and Yangkou had luck on their side; officials in Tangshan did not. Some of China's leading earthquake experts had gathered in Tangshan just a few weeks earlier for an "exchange of ideas on mass forecasting and precautionary work." Many of the scientists agreed the region between Beijing and Tangshan—some 180 kilometres—would be hit by a quake of magnitude 5 or 6 sometime that summer. Observable warning signs included quickly dropping water levels in wells, radon gas in water, and a change to atmospheric electricity readings. Disaster managers from Qinglong County jumped into action and convinced thousands of people to sleep outside in the days preceding the Great Tangshan Earthquake, saving many lives. But forecasting a medium quake sometime in the next few months in a vast geographical region is a far cry from specifying that a much larger quake will strike directly under a large industrial city. A prediction like that might have saved hundreds of thousands of lives in Tangshan. But it did not happen.

The catastrophe in Tangshan shook China's confidence in many of its leaders just a few months before Chairman Mao's death and called into question the belief that scientists could warn the public before an earthquake took place. Some scientists hoped the Tangshan disaster would lead to the obvious conclusion that earthquakes cannot be predicted. But some insisted that, even though the Tangshan disaster had exposed the difficulty, if not impossibility, of specific earthquake prediction, some level of prediction or forecasting might be possible in the future. Even if a precise time, location, and date could not be specified, these scientists argued, careful observations of geological phenomena could at least indicate broad time frames and locations where the risk of an earthquake was higher than usual.

In 1978 Japan enacted a law that allows its prime minister to issue an official alert if a six-member panel of experts believes a large-scale earthquake is imminent in the Tokai region. Japan's Meteorological Agency has installed instruments that measure strain in dozens of locations several hundred metres below the surface. If the bedrock expands or contracts at three or more of those locations, the panel meets. If they agree that a major quake is imminent, the prime minister has the power to take precautions like ordering evacuations and shutting down rail lines. This may be a sensible idea in a region that could lose millions of buildings and thousands of lives in the next big earthquake, but it's only practical if geological precursors allow for reliable short-term predictions, something many scientists insist is simply not possible. Some have been saying this ever since the law was first enacted. But the desire to see the disaster coming well in advance is a strong human impulse that is difficult to shake.

Charles Richter, the California seismologist and namesake of the Richter scale, was blunt about prediction. "Journalists and the general public rush to any suggestion of earthquake prediction," he lamented in 1977. "It provides a happy hunting ground for amateurs, cranks, and outright publicity-seeking fakers." True, but even some scientists have made earthquake prediction their domain. A focused experiment was conducted to test prediction in California in the 1980s. The San Andreas fault, near the town of Parkfield, produced six moderate earthquakes between 1857 and the mid 1980s—roughly one every twenty-two years. When scientists started their study, the most recent quake had occurred in 1966, so they did the math, so to speak, and calculated the likelihood of a similar quake striking before 1993 at 95 percent. Those calculations, according to the US Geological Survey, "now appear to have been oversimplified." In October 1992, a magnitude-4.7 quake near Parkfield put scientists and nearby residents on alert. Officials issued a seventy-two-hour public warning, putting the odds of a magnitude-6 event at 37 percent. The warning turned out to be a false alarm. There was no serious earthquake that year or even that decade.

In a very broad sense, the Parkfield prediction eventually proved right when a magnitude-6 earthquake rumbled out of that stretch of the San Andreas fault in 2004. The late arrival was of little comfort to proponents of prediction. They had already spent many years in vigorous debate with the skeptics. Robert J. Geller of the University of Tokyo is one of the most vocal critics of prediction. In 1997 he was the lead author of a provocative article in *Science* titled "Earthquakes Cannot Be Predicted." Geller called into question many of the claims made about the Haicheng earthquake, and he argued that there are simply too many variables to be able to predict with any accuracy. Seismologists' time and funding, he said, would be better spent on researching the longer-term recurrence rates and calculating intensities in specific areas to help with mitigation efforts.

Max Wyss, at the Geophysical Institute of the University of Alaska, turned Geller's argument on its head. Earthquake prediction doesn't divert funding from more important research, Wyss argued; quite the opposite. Too little funding has slowed further research into earthquake prediction, he complained in *Nature* in 1999. "The expression 'earthquake prediction' in a research proposal to the NSF or the USGS," he claimed, "will guarantee that it will not be funded." Millions of people already live and work in old buildings that are unlikely to be retrofitted before the next big earthquake, he noted. Improving our ability to forecast quakes will give many of these people a better chance of survival. The debate over whether or not research should focus on prediction dragged on for years. Then a different but related debate in Italy overshadowed it.

In 2009 a magnitude-6 temblor struck Italy's mountainous Abruzzo region just after 3:30 a.m. The epicentre was near the regional capital, L'Aquila. Foreshocks, the quake, and aftershocks devastated the thirteenth-century town and nearby villages, killing more than three hundred, injuring one thousand, and leaving sixty thousand homeless. Castles, cathedrals, and other historic buildings were destroyed. Relatively modern buildings also suffered significant damage: some of the concrete used in their construction was apparently poor quality, and the government threatened to prosecute any builders who had not adhered to seismic standards. It was a very different prosecution, however, that raised a new concern about earthquake prediction. Six scientists and one government official, members of the National Commission for the Forecast and Prevention of Major Risks, faced charges in connection with multiple deaths. Not only had they failed to predict the quake, prosecutors argued, but they had also reassured the people of L'Aquila that a deadly quake was unlikely, and they were therefore responsible for some of the lives lost.

Before the deadly quake, when tensions were running high in the region after strong foreshocks had rattled nerves, residents wondered if a big quake was coming. Many thought they should follow the centuries-old practice of sleeping outside. Others wanted expert advice, and who could blame them? Who would be eager to pitch a tent on the chance a big earthquake might strike on some unspeci-fied date in the future? Members of the National Commission faced intense pressure to do what they could not: provide a clear answer as to whether or not a major earthquake was about to strike the region. Bernardo De Bernardinis, a government official and the deputy head of the National Commission, told a journalist that the foreshocks rumbling in and around L'Aquila were releasing built-up pressure along the fault and making a large earthquake less likely. "The scientific community tells me there is no danger because there is an ongoing discharge of energy," he said. It is important to note that many scientists reject this theory, and the six who sat on the National Commission did not support De Bernardinis's assertion. Yet prosecutors charged them all with manslaughter, arguing that the six scientists had failed to denounce De Bernardinis's claim.

Scientist Alan I. Leshner, CEO of the American Association for the Advancement of Science, wrote to Giorgio Napolitano, the Italian president, to object to the prosecution of the scientists. "Years of research, much of it conducted by distinguished seismolo-gists in your own country," Leshner wrote, "have demonstrated that there is no scientific method for earthquake prediction that can be reliably used to warn citizens of an impending disaster. To expect more of science at this time is unreasonable. It is manifestly unfair for scientists to be criminally charged for failing to act on infor-mation that the international scientific community would consider inadequate as a basis for issuing a warning." Prosecutors, however, claimed the case was not about prediction but about the mischarac-terization of risk. Twenty-nine people, they claimed, stayed inside because of De Bernardinis's assurance. All seven commission mem-bers were convicted and sentenced to six-year prison terms. "It's incredible that scientists trying to do their job under the direction of a government agency have been convicted for criminal man-slaughter," Thomas Jordan, the director of the Southern California Earthquake Center, told *Science*.

The seven men appealed their convictions. Their lawyers argued that the scientists could not be held responsible for De Bernardinis's comment and that prosecutors had not established a causal link between the commission and the decision of some people in L'Aquila to stay inside on the night of the earthquake. "The only useful thing that can protect us from earthquakes," one appellant told the court, "is the seismic hazard map of a country. We showed a map where L'Aquila is purple, which means the highest hazard. That is what I said on 31 March 2009, and I would say the same thing today." The high-profile case took five years to wind its way through the Italian legal system. The Supreme Court of Cassation upheld De Bernardinis's conviction but reduced his sentence and acquitted the six scientists. "There is nothing to celebrate," said the director of the National Earthquake Centre, "because the pain of the people of L'Aquila remains."

It's a journalist's job to ask questions, and answering them is part of the job of many scientists. I've interviewed scientists and engineers about earthquakes for more than twenty years. At times it feels unfair, because simple questions do not necessarily lead to simple answers. It's reasonable to ask if earthquakes can be predicted, but the answer is not straightforward. And as the events following the L'Aquila earthquake prove, simple statements about earthquakes that have yet to happen can themselves carry risks.

Scientists in British Columbia do not know when the next Cascadia Subduction Zone megathrust quake will occur, but they do know when the odds go up. It happens pretty frequently. Scientists have used GPS technology to establish that Victoria is steadily moving towards the interior of British Columbia at a rate of about six millimetres a year. It doesn't sound like much, but it has added up to nearly two metres since the last major Cascadia Subduction Zone quake in 1700. The slow build in pressure appears to take a surprisingly regular break every fourteen to sixteen months, in episodes that scientists at the Geological Survey of Canada have named episodic tremor and slip, or ETS. These ETS episodes happen at a few subduction zones around the world. When they do, the fault slips loose deep beneath the surface, and the GPS data shows the surface moves backwards. Seismographs record clusters of silent tremors at the same time.

When I first interviewed seismologist John Cassidy at the Geological Survey of Canada about this, I presumed these episodes acted as a sort of release valve for the pressure building up in the rock. But the opposite is true: while the lower part of the fault slips, the upper part of the fault, which has been locked since the last great quake, continues to build up pressure. ETS does not help scientists predict earthquakes, but each episode "increases the likelihood of a great earthquake," according to the Geological Survey. "As the stress increases and approaches a critical level, an ETS event may provide the additional stress needed to overcome the friction on a fault, triggering a great earthquake." As more data is gathered, scientists may be able to provide better estimates of where and when the next Big One will take place. Then again, maybe they won't. The odds are higher that a massive quake will shake the ground during an ETS episode, but it could also happen in between episodes.

"Is prediction inherently impossible or just fiendishly difficult?" the University of Tokyo seismologist Robert J. Geller asked, before noting: "In practice, it doesn't matter."

THREE The East Coast

Chapter 9
BIG RISK IN THE BIG APPLE

Roughly three thousand people were on the Brooklyn Bridge on the afternoon of Sunday, August 10, 1884. The bridge had been popular with pedestrians since it opened fifteen months earlier. Elevated trains crossing the bridge slowed down as they approached the Park Row Terminus on the Manhattan side. Passengers exited the station on foot, dispersing in various directions. Many walked southwest, along Printing House Square, home to the great newspapers of the day: the *Sun, Tribune, Times,* and *World.* All stood cheek by jowl along Park Row, across the road from City Hall, and just a short dash to the courthouses, police headquarters, and the post office. This was before New York's skyscraper era, and the tallest structure at the time was the eighty-six-metre spire on Trinity Church.

Inside the five-storey *New York Times* building, the editorial team was discussing the next day's edition, unaware that the Coney Island earthquake was about to impose itself on the front page. Without warning, they heard a noise "like the rolling of tons of weight over the floor above." The rumbling sound quickly got louder, before there was a "sudden, sharp, convulsive quivering of the entire building." Editors wondered if someone had rolled the heavy printing forms in the composing room above them across the floor.

But press time was still many hours away, and the few men who were upstairs were not moving anything. Everyone stood in shocked silence as seismic waves rolled through the building. Window sashes rattled in their frames, and the thick pillars that stretched up to the roof seemed to quiver. "For a few seconds, the roof seemed about to fall," the *Times* reported. "An indescribable feeling of panic seized upon all."

In the eighty-metre-tall *New York Tribune* building the shaking was worse near the top of the nine stories of office space and stronger still in the clock tower above. "The shaking of the walls of high structures was terrible, because [it was] so sustained," the paper reported. "It was accompanied by a loud rumbling noise like the rushing of a heavily loaded wagon drawn by many horses over the pavement." In one tenth-floor flat, a young bachelor watched bottles and photographs fly off the shelves as the walls pitched side to side. "I started at first to run down stairs," he later told the *Sun*, "but I concluded that it would be as well for me to fall on the building as to have the building fall on me, so I stayed where I was."

The swaying motion was severe on the upper floors of tall buildings but no less terrifying in shorter buildings. Glass bottles in grocery shops flew off shelves and shattered, plates and mirrors smashed onto hotel floors, and the doorman at police headquarters thought thieves must have blown open the safe on the second floor. Out on the streets, people looked at each other in alarm and then looked "up at the buildings as though they expected them to topple over." Fruit vendors abandoned their sidewalk stands and bolted for the middle of the street. "You bet your life I ran!" one of them said. "I was looking down toward the bridge, and I could see the ground move. That was enough for me and I skipped." Half a mile to the north, on Ludlow and Essex Streets, people panicked and poured out of the crowded tenements "in the most abject terror." On the crowded sidewalks, people "seemed to reel like drunken men and clutch at the railings."

Across the city, a cacophony of sounds burst up and over the deep rumbling. At the Holmes Electric Protective Company, all 362 alarm bells wired to banks, stores, and other properties rang urgently. The employee on duty thought "Communists were up and were attacking the rich places of the city simultaneously." Men and women prayed out loud in the streets. Dozens fell to their knees in front of Trinity Church. A man getting his hair cut in a barber shop saw the barber's two stuffed birds jump up and down and thought they had come to life. At the Calvary Cemetery in Queens, a gravedigger was hard at work when the loose earth started to fall back into the fresh grave and gravestones threatened to topple over. He ran to the highway screaming, "It's the end of the world!"

Inside the lunatic asylum on Blackwell's Island, between Manhattan and Queens, patients were terrified. Prison guards in the nearby Blackwell's Island Penitentiary said the massive prison "trembled like an aspen," while prisoners 140 kilometres away in Camden, New Jersey, "begged to be released from their cells, as they were fearful of the building falling in upon them."

The shaking lasted for only about twenty seconds, but it left many New York residents trembling for hours. Some made their way to Printing House Square. This was nothing new; it was here that many New Yorkers first learned of significant events. Big crowds had gathered in the square twelve years earlier to hear that Ulysses S. Grant had defeated the founding editor of the *New York Tribune*, Horace Greeley, in his bid for the presidency. This time, the crowds gathered outside the newspaper offices heard more than just the facts. One quickly spreading rumour attributed the convulsions to a gas explosion that had killed one hundred people on the West Side. Others said an oil tank had exploded on Long Island. Both seemed plausible to some rattled New Yorkers who could scarcely believe an earthquake had just visited. One man drew a big crowd by "predicting emphatically that there would be a second shock at midnight." A few blocks away in the Western Union Telegraph office, reports streamed in of similar shocks from Maine to Pennsylvania, Washington to the Great Lakes.

Senator William M. Gwin of California was staying at the New York Hotel. "That is an earthquake!" the seventy-nine-year-old exclaimed, jumping into a doorway before the shaking stopped. He knew from long experience: "I was raised on 'em!" he later said. Gwin had first experienced an earthquake as a boy in the Mississippi River valley. He'd lived through severe shaking in Mexico in 1864 and a deadly quake in California four years later. Over at the Windsor Hotel, a California mining magnate named JC Flood quipped, "I see you New Yorkers are trying to imitate us, trying to put on style with earthquakes. But you can't get up a shake like we have in Frisco."

Geologists estimate the tremor was between magnitude 5.2 and magnitude 5.5. The quake was centred off Rockaway Beach, about twenty-seven kilometres southeast of New York City Hall. No one died as a direct result of the quake, though some reports blamed one death on fright. New Yorkers hoped that it was as strong a quake as they'd ever get, and the newspapers of the day tried to reassure them it was. "Of course it is impossible to prepare against earthquakes," the *Tribune* opined, "but we have reasonable assurance that this part of the earth's surface is not likely to be visited by them with any worse consequence than a general fright." The *Times* concurred: "those who look back upon the experience of yesterday, either with fear or with curiosity, may well rejoice that their lots are cast in a country where earthquakes do no harm."

Others were not so sure. The sergeant in charge of the local Signal Service Bureau, which would soon become the US Weather Bureau, wondered if the possibility of earthquakes should shape the future of New York. "If we are going to have earthquakes as regular visitors, we shall have to get rid of the tall buildings," he said. "If one of them gets cracked by a shock it will tumble down sure." To say he was ignored would put it mildly. New York was just starting its stunning vertical growth. The pressure to expand upwards was palpable. "Owners are generally putting up taller buildings, or changing those already erected, so as to give additional stories above the roofs of old-time structures," *Scientific American* noted in 1881.

By the summer of 1884, the Home Insurance Company had started construction of a ten-storey building in Chicago, which many would consider the world's first skyscraper. The fireproof iron, steel, and concrete structure was completed in 1885 and spurred a building boom in New York. In 1890 Joseph Pulitzer's World Building surpassed the Tribune Building when the dome on Pulitzer's new building reached ninety-four metres.

Today, New York has thousands of high-rises and skyscrapers. As a rule, these giant buildings are pretty strong. They have to be to withstand high winds and other stresses. But New York's streets are also lined with relatively low-rise brick buildings that are not as robust. Engineers worry this will be a problem in the future, when the ground under New York shakes as much it did back in 1884—or more.

"New York City has had the same hazard since Henry Hudson sailed up the Hudson River four hundred years ago," seismologist Lynn Sykes explains. "If you take the risk as hazard multiplied by assets, either people or structures, that's of course much higher today than it was in 1609." Sykes spent many years at Columbia University's Lamont–Doherty Geological Observatory (now the Lamont–Doherty Earth Observatory). He played a key role in the widespread acceptance of the plate tectonics theory and the American Geophysical Union recognized him for his "original contribution to the basic knowledge of the Earth's crust." Sykes has also been instrumental in nuclear-weapons testing and control, serving on the delegation that negotiated the Threshold Test Ban Treaty with the Soviet Union in the 1970s. He's also an authority on earthquake activity in and around New York, but he's received relatively little attention for this. The implications of rising sea levels get much more attention in New York than the risk of earthquakes, he observes. After all, the city hasn't had any deadly earthquakes in living memory, only a handful of small tremors that people could feel. But make no mistake: New York faces a real risk of suffering serious damage in an earthquake.

In many ways, New York City lies in an unlikely spot for earthquakes. It is located right in the middle of the giant North American plate and is a long way from tectonic boundaries. Still, that gigantic North American plate is being pushed to the west by the mid-oceanic ridge in the Atlantic and to the east by the San Andreas fault system on the Pacific Coast. And while most of the world's earthquakes take place along plate boundaries, the ground in the middle of massive plates sometimes shudders in events called intraplate earthquakes.

The rock under New York City is anywhere from 450 million to more than one billion years old. The intense heat and pressure of the Earth's crust has changed this ancient crystalline and metamorphic bedrock. In the process, it's developed brittle fractures and faults along its surface, which are prone to what geologists call offset. In other words, they can trigger earthquakes. The seismic potential for damaging earthquakes in New York City is real, veteran geologist Charles Merguerian insists. Merguerian has walked every block of Manhattan and walked or crawled through every tunnel under the city, except one machine-bored shaft that was simply too narrow for a man to fit inside. Along the way, he's mapped the geology and analyzed the faults, and what he's discovered has convinced him that the ground is capable of producing a much bigger shock than the 1884 quake. Merguerian points to the more devastating earthquake that flattened much of Charleston, South Carolina, in 1886. Scientists estimate that quake was anywhere from magnitude 6.9 to 7.3, or roughly one hundred times bigger and one thousand times stronger than the Coney Island quake.

"To me that geologic setting is no different from New York City," Merguerian says. "It's continental, exposed crustal rocks, over-lapped by coastal plains sediment. It's the same deal. So that to me would indicate the potential for that kind of earthquake."

Merguerian isn't the only scientist who has studied New York's geological footings and seen deadly seismic potential. For three decades, scientists at the Lamont–Doherty Earth Observatory cata-logued all 383 known earthquakes in a thirty-eight-thousand square kilometre area around New York City between 1677 and 2007. They assembled historical reports describing three hundred years of tremors, including evidence of two other earthquakes that matched the magnitude of the 1884 quake, one in 1737 and the other in 1783. They set up sensors in the 1970s and gathered thirty-four years of precise measurements of local ground movement, which often can't be felt at the surface. They've combined the modern data and the historic reports to confirm that some of the relatively small faults under New York City are still seismically active.

Historically, the few people in New York who paid any attention to what lay beneath the city presumed those fault lines were like-ly the remnants of continents that collided hundreds of millions of years ago. Construction crews and tunnel diggers have been unearthing old fractures for as long as people have been digging tunnels in the city. While the faults aren't as big as some in more seismically active regions, scientists who study them say an earth-quake in New York will likely do a lot more damage than the same magnitude quake in California. The geology of New York makes seismic activity more likely to happen near the surface, in the top mile or so, in the hard rock that's under a lot of the lower Hudson River Valley. The bedrock is so close to the surface in some places that New Yorkers can see it.

"If you walk across Central Park," Charles Merguerian says, "you're walking across an erosion surface that's been exhumed for probably twenty miles down. Twenty miles of rock have already been removed, and therefore we're exposing some ancient fracture-bearing crystalline rock that's very old, hard, and prone to brittle failure."

The Lamont–Doherty team's sensors have detected other, harder-to-find faults, especially outside the city, and discovered that many of these faults connect with previously identified regions, like the Ramapo Seismic Zone, which runs from eastern Pennsylvania to the mid–Hudson Valley and comes within a mile or two of the Indian Point nuclear facility. This is more of a fault zone than a single fault, one that includes an undetermined number of smaller veins that stretch out in many directions. The Ramapo Seismic Zone also has some troublesome neighbours. A set of almost parallel northwest-southeast faults, including Manhattan's 125th Street fault, generated a few small quakes in the 1980s and may have been the source of the 1737 earthquake.

Gathering more data about smaller, more frequent quakes lets researchers determine the approximate frequency of larger, more damaging ones. By measuring the length of faults and the size of tremors they create, and by observing how they store stress between shocks, seismologists can calculate how often the bigger ones happen. Based on the data collected so far, they estimate a magnitude-6 earthquake, which is ten times more powerful than a magnitude-5, will likely happen around every 670 years. This puts the likelihood of it happening in any fifty-year period at about 7 percent. The much more powerful magnitude-7 is estimated to occur every 3,400 years, or is roughly 1.5 percent likely in a fifty-year period. But a magnitude-6 earthquake under New York City would be devastating. The old, hard rock under much of the city tends to build up a lot of strain before it finally breaks, and researchers think short faults between one and ten kilometres long can cause magnitudes-5 and -6 quakes. Scientists estimate the magnitude-6 quakes strike on average every six hundred to seven hundred years, and they aren't sure when the last one took place. New York may not be overdue for a magnitude-6 earthquake, but the next one may not be a long way off, either.

A magnitude-6 quake directly under the United States' largest city would not feel at all moderate. It could damage big towers and major bridges, and it would probably devastate unreinforced brick buildings that are between three and six storeys tall. Many would sustain significant damage, and some would likely collapse. Outside the city, major infrastructure that crosses active fault lines, like the New York State Thruway, railroads, and gas and power lines, could be severed.

In 2003 the New York City Area Consortium for Earthquake Loss Mitigation released a report that tried to quantify the risk to the eighteen million people who live in the greater New York City area, which encompasses New York City, New Jersey, and Connecticut. A long list of emergency planners, scientists, and engineers from an equally long list of institutions that included FEMA, Columbia, Princeton, and many more city and state agencies took part. If a moderate magnitude-5.2 earthquake centred off-shore from Brooklyn happened, the study concluded, it would kill or injure only a few dozen people, but it would generate about 1.6 million tonnes of debris, the same amount that piled up when the Twin Towers collapsed.

Geological research suggests these magnitude-5 events strike the region every one hundred to two hundred years. The study estimated the likelihood of one happening in the next fifty years at between 20 and 40 percent. A moderate magnitude-6 quake would be much worse. If it struck at two o'clock in the afternoon, the study concluded, it would likely kill close to two thousand New Yorkers and send another two thousand to whatever hospitals remained standing and able to provide service. The study estimated that 2,600 buildings would be destroyed completely, and nine hundred fires would break out, which would kill more people. Nearly two hundred thousand people would be left homeless. And if the human suffering wasn't bad enough, the study estimated the cost at almost $40 billion. A magnitude-7 quake would cause almost $200 billion in damage, destroy more than twelve thousand buildings, and lead to more than 6,700 deaths. "Considering the area's historic seismicity, population density, and vulnerability of the region's built environment," the study's authors wrote, "it is clear that even a moderate earthquake would have a significant impact on the lives and economy of the Tri-State region."

The report paints a frightening picture of New York's vulnerability, especially in Manhattan, but some scientists worry more about the potential impact on nuclear facilities. The Indian Point Energy Center is a nuclear power plant located just thirty-eight kilometres north of New York; it's the closest nuclear facility to a major US city. In 2010, the Nuclear Regulatory Commission ranked it the most likely of all 104 reactors in the United States to suffer reactor core damage in an earthquake, pegging the chance of damage to the core of reactor 3 at one in ten thousand in any given year. By comparison, the Diablo Canyon Power Plant, which is located between San Francisco and Los Angeles and is the only remaining nuclear plant operating in California, was given odds of one in twenty-three thousand.

The first Indian Point nuclear reactor was built in the 1960s and was shut down in 1974 because, as the regulatory commission put it, "the emergency core cooling system did not meet regulatory requirements." Concerns about a possible earthquake didn't really come to light until that year, when the owner applied to build two more reactors. Lynn Sykes remembers the New York State Geological Survey and the State of New York became involved, worried that "the Indian Point reactors were not designed for a large earthquake."

At first, the commission used only the largest "historical earthquake" as a benchmark, looking just at earthquakes that had occurred since Europeans settled in the area in the 1600s, the largest of which was about magnitude 5. The New York Geological Survey and the state government convinced the regulators to raise their standards to magnitude 7, although they had pushed for designs that would prepare for magnitude 8. Sykes notes that both Eastern Canada and New England have experienced some intensity-8 earthquakes and thinks it would be a good idea to prepare for that possibility.

A scientific consensus on the biggest earthquake that could strike the New York City area does not exist, but some lawmakers felt Indian Point was unsafe and needed to close. Before he was elected New York's fifty-sixth governor, Andrew Cuomo served as the state's attorney general. He was already concerned about the safety of Indian Point in 2007, when Lamont–Doherty data about the fault zone around the plant was shared with his office. Researchers had discovered a new active seismic zone running from Stamford, Connecticut, to Peekskill, New York, that connected with the Ramapo Seismic Zone just a few kilometres from the Indian Point Energy Center. The Stamford–Peekskill line runs roughly parallel to faults that start at 125th Street and that scientists believed could produce a deadly earthquake. They suspected the Stamford–Peekskill line could as well.

In the fall of 2007, Cuomo told the Nuclear Regulatory Commission that new data disclosed a "substantially higher likelihood of significant earthquake activity" near Indian Point, activity that could "exceed the earthquake design for the facility." The owner of the plant, Entergy, had not presented new earthquake data since 1979 and had not taken into account the heightened risk from the previously unknown crossroads of two active seismic zones.

Some scientists doubt the level of risk near Indian Point. Alan Kafka, the director of Boston College's Weston Observatory, considered the Lamont–Doherty research an "interesting but still speculative hypothesis" about the seismic zone between Peekskill and Stamford. Kafka acknowledged the earthquake hazard in the greater New York area but argued that scientists knew relatively little about earthquakes in and around New York City. "The impression is given once again that our understanding of the relationship between faults and earthquakes in this region is clear when in fact it isn't." Nonetheless, Andrew Cuomo and the environmental group Riverkeeper were convinced the risk was too high and that Indian Point needed to be closed. In 2017, Governor Cuomo finally announced what he'd been waiting fifteen years to say: Entergy would close the two remaining reactors at Indian Point by 2021. Entergy cited the growing supply of cheap natural gas. Cuomo boasted the closure "eliminates a major risk, provides welcome relief, and New Yorkers can sleep a little better."

It seems logical that closing nearby reactors should reduce the nuclear risk to New York City. The reactors themselves, however, aren't the only source of potential nuclear contamination. That's because the spent nuclear fuel might remain at the site for years or even decades. Riverkeeper claims Indian Point has one of the largest stocks of spent, or irradiated, fuel in the United States: more than 1,500 tonnes in 2019.

Nuclear fuel eventually runs out of energy, and when it does it needs to be removed from the reactor and replaced with fresh fuel. Spent nuclear fuel is so hot, thermally and radioactively, that it's stored inside the reactors, often for a few years, and then moved into specially designed spent-fuel storage pools. These pools, often twelve metres or deeper, hold the discarded fuel until it cools down enough that it can be moved to dry storage. The water in the pool is cooled continually and acts as both a thermal coolant and a radiation shield.

The nuclear industry has long claimed this a safe process — a claim that events at the Fukushima Daiichi power plant in Japan undermined when the tsunami waves knocked out the emergency diesel generators that powered the plant's cooling systems.

Temperatures inside each reactor rose and triggered hydrogen gas explosions that destroyed the buildings that covered reactors 1, 2, and 3. Luckily, the spent fuel in those storage pools remained underwater. Reactor 4 was densely packed with spent fuel and the Tokyo Electric Power Company underestimated the evaporation rate of the water surrounding it. A month after the disaster, when officials could finally get to the pool to inspect it, they discovered the water had fallen from seven metres to two. Luckily, water from the adjacent reactor cavity had leaked into the pool and helped prevent a fire. If a fire had broken out, American scientists at Sandia National Laboratories estimated the release of cesium-137 into the atmosphere would have been one hundred times greater than it was. That could have forced between 1.6 and 35 million people to relocate from Japan's east coast.

The Fukushima disaster raised a number of worrying possibilities for nuclear regulators. The US Nuclear Regulatory Commission reviewed many of its safety practices and ultimately adopted a number of improvements, but it decided not to impose higher standards on the management of spent nuclear fuel, and that worries some scientists. If the spent-fuel pools crack in an earthquake, will radiation leak into the atmosphere? The nuclear industry insists the chance of that happening is extremely low, because spent fuel is nowhere near the potency of new fuel. They also claim nothing in the pool could trigger a chain reaction.

Their reassurances don't satisfy everyone. Alison Macfarlane is a geologist who was the chair of the Nuclear Regulatory Commission from 2012 to 2014. The events in Fukushima were still fresh when she started, and she hoped the commission would investigate what happened in Japan and review whether or not the United States needed stricter regulations around spent nuclear fuel. "It could be that the situation is fine and nothing needs to change," she says. "Or it could be that the situation is not fine, and that new calculations show there are periods of vulnerability when you need a different kind of plan. But you shouldn't make decisions in a vacuum; you should make decisions based on data. I think it would have been worthwhile for the Nuclear Regulatory Commission to collect that data."

The Nuclear Regulatory Commission did not collect that data, which leaves Macfarlane concerned about the storage of spent nuclear fuel. The commission, she says, does not require nuclear power companies to show regulators when or how they discharge fuel or how they get it into the storage pools. And, perhaps most importantly, plant operators are not required to tell the regulator how much spent fuel is stored on site. That's important, because it means the Nuclear Regulatory Commission doesn't know how much excess-storage capacity each nuclear plant has at any given moment, and it doesn't require them to maintain what they call full-core offload. "There are a few reactors in the US that do not maintain that core amount of space," Macfarlane explains. "So were there to be an emergency where they had to take all the fuel from the core, they would have a real problem," because they wouldn't have anywhere safe to store the radioactive material. When Macfarlane was still chair, she thought the commission should set density requirements for spent-fuel pools that would prevent plant operators from leaving too little spare room. "They started to," she says, "then they stopped. And I tried to convince them otherwise, but my colleagues on the commission did not agree."

Macfarlane insists she has great faith in the scientists and staff at the Nuclear Regulatory Commission, but too many decisions about nuclear regulation are influenced by politics and the nuclear industry, which doesn't share much information with the public. A concerned citizen can't find out if Indian Point, or any other plant in a seismically active zone, is maintaining enough space for all of the reactor's fuel, because the commission doesn't track that information.

In 2017 researchers from Princeton University and the Union of Concerned Scientists published an article in *Science* that claimed American nuclear regulators were underestimating the risk that a nuclear disaster could start in spent-fuel pools. They singled out the Nuclear Regulatory Commission's failure to end the dense packing of spent-fuel pools, "which we consider critical for avoiding a potential catastrophe much greater than Fukushima. Unless the NRC improves its approach to assessing risks and benefits of safety improvements—by using more realistic parameters in its quantitative assessments and also taking into account societal impacts—the United States will remain needlessly vulnerable to such disasters." Their warning bears an ominous similarity to the condemnations of Japanese lawmakers after the Fukushima disaster. Japan's legislature, the National Diet, assembled a Nuclear Accident Independent Investigation Commission to learn from the tragedy. The chair of the commission, Kiyoshi Kurokawa, concluded that a nuclear accident did not have to follow the earthquake and tsunami of 2011, calling what happened at the plant "a profoundly manmade disaster," one "that could and should have been foreseen and prevented."

Eliminating the risk of a nuclear catastrophe will likely require the creation of a national repository for the dry storage of spent fuel rods, and the long effort to build a deep geological dry storage space under Yucca Mountain, in Nevada, is currently stalled. In the meantime, many nuclear plant operators simply store their dry spent fuel in steel and concrete casks on site. Thousands of tonnes of spent fuel is stored at nuclear facilities across the United States. Of particular concern is the Peach Bottom plant, on the banks of the Susquehanna River between Philadelphia and Baltimore. The Nuclear Regulatory Commission's post-Fukushima study concluded a spent-fuel fire in a densely packed pool at Peach Bottom could force the evacuation of an area covering 24,500 square kilometres, affecting four million people. If the Peach Bottom storage tanks remain crowded, researchers from Princeton and the Union of Concerned Scientists estimate the number of evacuees could be as many as twenty million—five times higher than the NRC projection.

Even if the nuclear risk is removed completely, plenty of seismic safety concerns in New York will remain. While Seattle, Portland, and Vancouver were late to wake up to their earthquake risk, New York City slept in even later. The city only included seismic standards in its building code in 1995. As a result, thousands of unreinforced masonry buildings crowd New York City. Manhattan is at the greatest risk, being home to almost thirty thousand of these vulnerable structures. The Upper East Side, with its soft soils, is especially vulnerable. The softer ground amplifies the shaking so much that the peak ground acceleration could be nearly twice as strong in the Upper East Side as in the Financial District, which stands on more solid rock. The Upper East Side also has nearly four times as many unreinforced masonry buildings as the Financial District. This affluent neighbourhood is farther away from the epicentre of the 1884 earthquake, but it's at much higher risk. If a magnitude-6 earthquake strikes, scientists estimate 2,600 buildings will be completely destroyed. While San Francisco and Los Angeles have for many years required the strengthening of old brick buildings, New York has made no such demands of the owners of its old buildings.

Beautiful old brownstones make up about 80 percent of the housing stock in some Brooklyn neighbourhoods and are an icon of the borough. Many of them date back to the 1860s, when new mining methods made sandstone cheaper than granite, limestone, or marble. But brownstones often stand on foundations made of rubble or brick, their walls lack reinforcement, and there are no connections between the walls and the floors. Many of these buildings withstood the 1884 quake. But if the next quake is stronger, they will crumble.

Researchers from the New York University School of Engineering estimate the cost of strengthening a five-storey brownstone at

$175,000. That's only a small fraction of the cost of building one brand new — and of its current value — but still a considerable expense for many owners. Cost could well be one reason so few brownstones have received seismic renovations, but it's not the only one. Most owners just don't know about the risk. "People in New York don't think about it," Charles Merguerian laments. "They just don't think about it."

Chapter 10
CHARLESTON AND OTHER EAST COAST QUESTIONS

·

The 1880s were a seismically active decade on the Eastern Seaboard. Charleston, the oldest city in South Carolina, was a busy port in 1886, and one that had already endured significant hardship. Hurricanes, fires, regular outbreaks of malaria and smallpox, and two wars had brought a good deal more death and destruction to Charleston than many cities ever face. None of those miseries was greater than the suffering of the generations of slaves who passed through the city. Charleston was the largest slave port in the United States, and for more than a century it was the entry point for nearly half of all Africans shipped against their will across the Atlantic Ocean. Historians estimate more than one hundred thousand slaves first set foot in America on Gadsden's Wharf, just a mile from Charleston City Hall.

After the Civil War, many freed slaves remained in Charleston, and by the 1880s just over half of the city's population of sixty thousand people was black. They lived in a city that was still rebuilding from the ravages of war, which included a giant fire that destroyed nearly six hundred buildings. "I doubt any city was ever more terribly punished than Charleston," General William Tecumseh Sherman remarked, "but as her people had for years been agitating for war and discord, and had finally inaugurated the Civil War, the judgement of the world will be that Charleston deserved the fate that befell her." While many if not all white Charlestonians would deny they were to blame, no one questioned that Charleston suffered extreme hardship during the war. But more was to come.

In August 1885, one of the most violent hurricanes on record subjected Charleston to even more destruction. "The streets of Charleston were not more desolate at the end of two hours than after the bombardment during the war," one reporter observed. The hurricane completely destroyed wharves and warehouses along the waterfront, which had only recently been rebuilt. Cotton presses, churches, lumber mills, and homes suffered extensive damage.

By the following August, Charleston was in the grips of a stifling heat wave and still rebuilding from what locals called "that terrible cyclone." Many businesses shut their doors in the hot afternoons and reopened in the cooler evening hours. On August 31, a significant number of Charleston residents were just returning home for the night when the quake struck shortly before ten o'clock. "It came lightly with a gentle vibration of the houses as when a cat trots across the floor," survivor Paul Pinckney recalled twenty years later. "But a very few seconds of this, and it began to come in sharp jolts and shocks which grew momentarily more violent until buildings were shaken as toys." Inside the offices of the *News and Courier*, "the tremor was now a rude, rapid quiver that agitated the whole lofty strong-walled building as though it were being shaken by the hand of an immeasurable power with an intent to tear its joints asunder and scatter its stones and bricks abroad."

Panicked people fled their houses in terror, and falling bricks claimed several lives. Those who survived found themselves shrouded in the darkness of a choking cloud of dust from the lime mortar and shattered masonry. The shaking lasted almost a minute, and the silence that followed was brief. "The sound of helpless, horror-stricken humanity, old, young, strong and feeble alike, where all are feeble, calling for help from their fellow creatures, and raising their anguished voice to Heaven for mercy, where no human aid could avail," rose in the darkness. Some survivors braved teetering buildings to drag out the bedridden on their mattresses. Many of those vulnerable people were then left to fend for themselves in the chaos.

Frequent and frightening aftershocks meant the compositors at the *News and Courier* could not print a newspaper, but its reporters sent vivid descriptions of the event to the *Savannah Morning News* to publish. "It is not a scene to be described by any mortal tongue," the paper declared. "It is not a scene to be forgotten when it has been witnessed and when a witness has shared all its dangers." As the tremors continued into the night, fires broke out. The main gas lines were so damaged and the joints to smaller lines so strained that gas leaks and fires were inevitable. Within hours, buildings across the city were in flames, but the terror visited upon Charlestonians by the earthquake was so intense that many people scarcely noticed the fiery glow. "No one watched the ruddy flames or pillars of cloud rising high into the still night air," the *Savannah Morning News* reported. "All were too intent on listening with strained senses for the dreaded recurrence of that horrible growl or groan of the power under the seas and under the land to give thought to new terrors, though it had threatened many homes in the doomed city." Hordes of rats and mice streamed out of houses across the shattered city.

When the sun rose, the survivors discovered that many patches of ground had liquefied at seemingly random locations. Sand blows had erupted across the city, spouting sand and water like mini volcanoes. People passing the iconic St. Michael's Church, which had remained standing through both the American Revolution and the Civil War, may have noticed that its large clock, in a tower seventy-seven stairs above the street, was stuck at 9:51, the precise time when the earthquake struck the city.

Outside Charleston, railroad tracks and trestles were twisted and bent and several trains had derailed. Fissures had opened up and were visible in the ground, one of which measured six hundred metres long. Water from collapsed dams flooded fields and roads. The quake was felt over a huge area, from Cuba in the south to New York in the north, the Mississippi River in the west, and Bermuda in the east. Up and down the coast, telegraph wires started buzzing almost immediately after the quake, transmitting reports of violent shaking. Operators soon noticed the absence of dispatches from Charleston: the city's telegraph lines, like so much else, had collapsed.

Scientists now estimate the quake was as large as magnitude 7.3. The Charleston Health Department reported twenty-seven people were killed on the night of the quake and another forty-nine died from quake-related illness or injury in the month that followed. The increasingly wet, cold, and unsanitary conditions in the city's overcrowded relief camps claimed lives. Social historian Richard N. Côté examined newspaper reports from South Carolina and surrounding states in the months following the quake and counted 124 separate deaths attributed to the quake. As is often the case in natural disasters, the poor suffered disproportionately. Though the city's population was split roughly evenly between the races, 73 percent of the officially recorded deaths were black.

Thousands of people sustained injuries: broken bones, sprained or dislocated knees and hips, fractured skulls from falling debris. Many victims had their arms or legs crushed so badly that amputation was the only option. Treating the injured, clearing debris, and repairing infrastructure were not Charleston's only challenges. Thousands of suddenly homeless people needed food and shelter. A few days after the initial quake, with aftershocks still terrorizing residents, roughly forty thousand people were sleeping in streets or parks. Citizens fearful of returning to their damaged homes used railroad boxcars and cargo ships as shelter. Some slept in stables; others stripped ships of their sails to make tents.

Countless survivors suffered what would now be diagnosed as

post-traumatic stress disorder. Many traumatized residents managed the psychological trauma with the help of Charleston's saloons, which opened mere hours after the quake. Others counted on doctors and pharmacists to provide them with sedatives. Laudanum, valerian, and morphine were all in high demand. Other cases were much more severe. Some lost their hair. Others simply walked out of the city in a daze. Some required institutionalization. The *News and Courier* profiled a number of city residents who were sent to the South Carolina Lunatic Asylum in Columbia, including a four-teen-year-old girl: "The shock of Tuesday completely shattered her mind, and she is now raving with a strong homicidal tendency." Newspapers reported a rash of suicides. The *Atlanta Constitution* described some of these tragic deaths in considerable detail. One victim used a .38-calibre pistol, and three others jumped off a bridge.

Most people who have never experienced an earthquake have an intrinsic trust that the ground they stand on will stay put. That trust is common in cities where people have no living memory of earthquakes, and in North America that includes most cities. But maybe it shouldn't. While most earthquakes happen along the boundaries between tectonic plates, they also happen in the middle of plates, hundreds of kilometres from where the tectonic action usually occurs. The earthquakes that struck New York in 1884 and Charleston in 1886 were both intraplate quakes. If those two cities can shake, there's reason to wonder if some of their neighbours can, too. Seismologists admit they don't fully know where damaging intraplate earthquakes can occur.

In 2011 an earthquake shook Washington, DC. The event was centred near Mineral, Virginia, 140 kilometres southwest of the American capital. It was a serious quake emanating from a fault zone that scientists didn't even know about at the time. Though the magnitude-5.8 earthquake was centred near a town of fewer than five hundred, millions of people felt it. It was the biggest seismic event to hit the eastern states since 1944, when another magnitude-5.8 temblor struck along the Canada–United States border, near Cornwall, Ontario, and Massena, New York.

The 2011 quake happened in the afternoon, but it was a wake-up call. The tremors cracked the top of the pyramid on the Washington Monument and the flying buttresses and spires of the Washington National Cathedral. The quake also raised alarmed questions about how much damage a slightly stronger jolt would inflict. Although no one was killed or seriously injured, the shaking caused tens of millions of dollars in damage and rattled confidence. The intensity surprised many people, given that the epicentre of this moderate earthquake was relatively far from the capital.

Geophysicist Thomas Pratt at the US Geological Survey decided to investigate. He led a team that installed more than two dozen seismic monitors in and around Washington in 2014. Over the course of ten months, the instruments recorded thirty small earthquakes and revealed an important component of seismic risk: the shaking was amplified in the parts of the city built on top of thin, loose layers of sediment; buildings on harder, stronger bedrock felt considerably less movement.

The quake caused significant worry beyond Washington. It was felt from Maine down to Georgia and as far west as Chicago, a land mass that is home to roughly a third of the US population. That's the thing about earthquakes in eastern North America: they travel about ten times farther than similarly sized quakes west of the Rockies, probably because the older, denser rock allows seismic waves to travel more efficiently. That's led some scientists to wonder if other American cities might be at risk, especially those that sit on soil structure similar to Washington's. The ground under the cities of Baltimore, Maryland; Richmond, Virginia; and Trenton, New Jersey, is also composed of soft sedimentary soil on top of hard bedrock. While all fifty states have a potential for earthquakes, sixteen states have experienced a magnitude-6 or greater quake in the past: all three West Coast states plus Alaska, Hawaii, Arkansas, Idaho,

Kentucky, Missouri, Montana, Nevada, South Carolina, Tennessee, Texas, Utah, and Wyoming. The US Geological Survey says forty-two states are reasonably likely to experience one in the future. Seismologist Lynn Sykes believes the lack of scientific understanding about earthquakes in eastern North America—about exactly where they occur and why they happen in certain places—is significant. "I think that Boston and Providence, Rhode Island, and Philadelphia need more concern," he says, "because we just don't understand the occurrence of eastern earthquakes."

New England's history offers reports of a few damaging earthquakes in the decades since the first British settlers arrived. Boston College seismologist John Ebel estimates a 1638 temblor centred near Concord, New Hampshire, may have been as big as magnitude 7. A 1755 offshore quake near Cape Ann, Massachusetts, was likely magnitude 6.2. Ebel theorizes that modern earthquakes in New England may in fact be "very late aftershocks of earthquakes that took place hundreds or thousands of years ago." The uncertainty about his theory is considerable, but scientists agree that Boston could suffer terrible damage if a quake of that magnitude shook New England today. Like Charleston, many of Boston's older city neighbourhoods are built on fill. Thousands of unreinforced masonry buildings stand on what used to be marshland or shallow water. A 2004 study established a significant threat of liquefaction following a strong earthquake in and around Back Bay, South Boston, the Cambridge waterfront, and Logan Airport.

If nothing else, emergency planners in South Carolina now have more information to work with, thanks in large part to Charleston's 1886 earthquake. The South Carolina Emergency Management Division commissioned a study in 2012 that rated the likelihood the state will experience a damaging earthquake sometime in the next fifty years as relatively high. If a magnitude-7 earthquake struck the state today, the study estimates nine hundred people would die, nine thousand would suffer serious injuries, and about two hundred thousand would be left homeless, at least temporarily. Hundreds of thousands of households would lose their power and running water, and hundreds of hospitals, fire stations, and schools would be knocked out of commission. In total, the study predicts a South Carolina quake would cost the state economy roughly $20 billion. That quake could be a few hundred years away, but a smaller quake, around magnitude 6, could also cause serious problems. "It would be pretty bad," says Charleston seismologist Steven Jaume. "A lot of the infrastructure around here is old."

As with so many other cities, the large number of unreinforced masonry buildings poses a serious safety risk in Charleston. More than 1,200 brick buildings were damaged in the 1886 earthquake. Good mortar contains gravel with rough edges, to form a strong bond, and lime, which in South Carolina often came from burnt oyster shells. Post-quake inspections revealed that many buildings built with strong mortar had fared well. Many of the brick buildings that had collapsed, however, had been built with mortar that was little better than mud; in essence, sand and gravity held the bricks together. A large proportion of Charleston's buildings were made with this inferior mortar. The problem started after a massive fire in 1838 consumed more than one thousand wood buildings in a single day. In response, the city required that all new buildings in that area be built of brick. A rush of opportunistic builders flooded into Charleston, and a rash of poorly constructed brick buildings followed them. Many of those buildings, erected so quickly after the 1838 fire, fell apart in the 1886 quake. And the potential for history to repeat itself is ominous: in the heroic effort to rebuild the city after 1886, reporters and engineers who observed the reconstruction noted the use of poor-quality mortar. Many of the brick structures that withstood the 1886 quake had been made using a pattern called Flemish bond, in which every brick alternated between sitting lengthwise and sitting sideways. Another strong method was the English bond, which sandwiched rows of bricks laid lengthwise

CHARLESTON AND OTHER EAST COAST QUESTIONS

in between rows of bricks laid sideways. Both methods seemed to ensure greater stability and ensure a good deal of mortar would adhere to each and every brick. In contrast, some of the slapdash rebuilding efforts laid almost all the bricks lengthwise in what is sometimes called American bond.

Efforts have been made to strengthen some of these fragile old structures. Some received an early form of seismic retrofit that consisted of horizontal steel rods and bolts, called tie rods and pattress plates, installed through the floors from one wall to the other in an effort to hold the building together. Those bolts are still visible on many exterior brick walls in Charleston, but they have never really been tested, and engineers can't agree on whether the rudimentary fixes will do more harm than good in a serious earthquake.

Even if old brick buildings don't collapse completely, many could lose their brick facades. The historic and charming King Street shopping district has many old masonry facades that could detach from the buildings in even moderate shaking. Depending on the time and day of a future earthquake, a cascade of bricks could shower down on shoppers below, as happened on Colombo Street in Christchurch in 2010. Despite the risk, Charleston does not require regular inspections of facades, even though facade connectors can weaken over time. Other cities have put a higher priority on prevention: Pittsburgh requires the inspection of all facades every five years, while Chicago requires inspection every five years for high-rises more than fifty years old. The charming old structures that make Charleston so appealing to tourists could spell disaster in the future. "They were repaired," Steven Jaume says. "The question is, how well will those repairs hold up if something happens again?"

The answer to that question may depend as much on the ground underneath those brick buildings as the quality of their construction. Many of the city's most vulnerable buildings stand on especially shaky ground. Charleston sits on a peninsula between two rivers that is criss-crossed by several tidal creeks. As the city grew in the eighteenth and nineteenth centuries, a mix of garbage, building waste, and sand was used to fill in creek beds and marshes. By 1886 roughly 40 percent of the buildings in the city sat on what Charlestonians call made land. During the 1886 quake, soft soils liquefied and amplified the shaking so significantly that buildings on made land suffered more damage than those on hard ground.

And the problem only worsened in the months after the earthquake, when the debris from thousands of damaged buildings was hauled away and dumped into local ponds and tidal creeks in the western parts of Charleston, creating even more unstable land. A decade later, that reclaimed land was used for new construction, and buildings on those lots today are highly vulnerable to liquefaction. In fact, Steven Jaume says, many of the suburbs in what is now one of America's fastest-growing cities are "basically the areas that liquefied in 1886." Charleston is much more densely populated than it was in 1886: more than eight hundred thousand people now call the metropolitan area home. While many new buildings built after seismic codes were strengthened in the 1980s would perform well on solid ground, the loose soils beneath some of them could undermine the engineering improvements that should make them safe.

Soft soils aren't the only issue. For some buildings, something as simple as orientation can make a fatal difference. Rectangular buildings oriented to the east and west suffered more damage in the 1886 earthquake than rectangular buildings oriented north and south (square buildings are typically stronger). That's because seismic waves travelled north to south through the long walls of east-west buildings, putting more stress on those buildings than their perpendicular neighbours. James Stevenson Lyles, an architectural conservator in Charleston, believes "east-west buildings likely failed more due to their orientation to the earthquake's epicentre." But the epicentre of the next big earthquake could be somewhere else along the fault, meaning the seismic waves could move in other directions. Owners cannot rely on a building's orientation as any sort of insurance. The long walls of all rectangular unreinforced masonry buildings require strengthening, no matter their orientation.

In his master's thesis in historical preservation, Lyles urged the city to compile an inventory of unreinforced masonry buildings that prioritizes buildings based on their date of construction, type of brick-bond used, location, and soil type. As of 2020, however, Charleston has no seismic retrofit requirements for older buildings, and there isn't a lot of discussion about them, either. Steven Jaume says the lack of seismic preparedness is understandable in a city where people have more pressing concerns, like hurricanes and flooding from rising sea levels. Like many low-lying coastal communities, Charleston is seeing the early effects of climate change, and every weekday before his morning commute, Jaume checks the local tide tables, because the quickest route to work is also the one that can flood at high tide. In recent years, he's counted fifty days of tidal flooding on sunny blue-sky days. Throw in the occasional tornado watch, and Jaume thinks Charleston residents can be forgiven for not being preoccupied with an earthquake that may or may not strike in their lifetime: "People can only pay attention to so much."

Chapter 11

UN VIOLENT TREMBLEMENT DE TERRE

Ottawa, Ontario, isn't often thought of as earthquake country, but in 2010 a magnitude-5 quake rumbled out of the Laurentian Mountains, fifty-six kilometres north of the city. The shaking lasted for around thirty seconds and was the biggest quake to hit Canada's capital in sixty-five years. Chimneys collapsed, windows shattered at city hall, and cracks appeared in the walls of Parliament Hill's press gallery. Government buildings were evacuated and staff sent home for the day. Senators had to move out onto the lawn to adjourn proceedings formally. Jay Hill, a Conservative MP from British Columbia, stood outside the East Block and looked back at its gothic sandstone walls and copper roof. The tremor felt, he said, like a large bulldozer had gone by.

A portion of highway collapsed near Val-des-Boies, and Geneviève Blais, who was at home on the shores of Hawk Lake, about five kilometres away from the epicentre, said it felt "like someone set off dynamite below us." Ninety kilometres to the north of Ottawa, people in the town of Gracefield, Quebec, panicked. "Employees were crying," Réal Rochon, Gracefield's mayor, recalled. "They were sent home." The town hall, a church, and a restaurant suffered serious damage. Mayor Rochon declared a state of emergency and asked for provincial and federal assistance. In Montréal, the 911 system received a deluge of calls, though no serious injuries were reported. In Toronto, fire alarms rang in the city's tall towers, and many offices were evacuated temporarily.

The quake originated in the southern portion of the Western Quebec Seismic Zone, which produces frequent small tremors. In an average year, 150 earthquakes are recorded in the region. Most are too small for people to notice them, but from time to time, the seismic zone produces moderate earthquakes that can cause major damage if they're close to cities and towns.

That's a particular concern in areas composed largely of old brick buildings, like the historic ByWard Market district in downtown Ottawa. The neighbourhood's low-rise masonry buildings house cafés, restaurants, brewpubs, and quite a few walk-up apartment buildings. Most were built several decades before Canada's building code required reinforcements.

"These masonry buildings are like pieces of chalk," Murat Saatcioglu, a professor of civil engineering at the University of Ottawa, explains. "You want to bend them, but they can't. If you force it, they break. There's no reinforcement, nothing connecting them." Saatcioglu says buildings in Ottawa and western Quebec that were designed after the mid-1980s are typically earthquake-resistant. Anything older could be a risk, especially low- and mid-rise buildings, because the frequency of ground-shaking in the region tends to match the natural movement of buildings of that height. In a typical Ottawa earthquake, the ground would take between one-fifth of a second and a full second to shake one way and back, and that timing matches the natural frequency of buildings anywhere between two and ten storeys. "If the period of excitation matches the period of the building," Saatcioglu explains, "then a phenomenon called resonance occurs, so they start vibrating vigorously."

The Geological Survey of Canada and the University of Ottawa's Hazard Mitigation and Disaster Management Research Centre assessed Ottawa's building stock. In 2014 Amid El Sabbagh, a graduate student in civil engineering, conducted a detailed assessment of sixteen brick buildings in downtown Ottawa and concluded three of them had a very high risk of structural collapse. He also took a broad look at the city's building stock as a whole. He concluded nearly three-quarters of the buildings in the downtown core were built before 1940 and should be assessed for seismic safety. Of the 1,500 old brick buildings he identified, more than half of them stood on soft soils that would increase shaking significantly in a strong earthquake. Overall he concluded about a third of the old unreinforced masonry buildings would be at or near collapse in the level of shaking that the building code now considers when establishing seismic standards. He also looked at 580 reinforced concrete buildings and concluded most of them would suffer little or no damage.

Taller buildings are less prone to damage from shaking than shorter buildings, at least in the type of earthquake that might strike Ottawa. Row housing is also thought to be more robust because the multiple shared walls offer more support. Overall, the most vulnerable structures seem to be old stand-alone low- or mid-rise brick buildings. But appearances can be deceiving, and some of those squat brick boxes can be pretty robust. The Geological Survey of Canada, home to much of Canada's geophysical and earthquake monitoring, is based in a three-level red-brick block that was built just before the First World War. The building has a steel infrastructure that should hold it together when an earthquake finally strikes the source of so much seismic research.

John Adams, the seismologist who played a pivotal role in identifying the risk of the Cascadia Subduction Zone in the 1980s, works in this brick building and doesn't lose sleep worrying about when the next major earthquake will strike Ottawa. But, he concedes, the city will suffer. He expects a lot of buildings will probably fall down if they're close to a strong earthquake strike and that everyone will probably say the risk is unacceptable — at least after the fact. The more important question right now, Adams says, is what should the city do about it? Like so many other vulnerable cities, Ottawa has not forced property owners to make vulnerable buildings safer. The city has other concerns, like tornadoes and, its top natural threat, ice storms, which can cut off power at a time of year when people need it most. Pierre Poirier, the city's head of emergency management, worries some of his fellow citizens underestimate the risk that earthquakes pose. Even a quake with a relatively low number on the Richter scale, he says, could have a devastating impact. "Whenever we have a small tremor it gets a little bit of a profile, but overall it probably doesn't have the significant profile that it should."

Like others, Poirier points to the large stock of old brick buildings as a concern. But he also worries about newer homes in suburbs like Orleans, which are built on unstable ground. Some neighbourhoods are built on deposits of Leda clay, also known as quick clay. Leda clay can amplify shaking by as much as six times during an earthquake. When it's stressed that much the clay can liquefy, and even new structures built to modern seismic standards can tip over, sink, or slide down a slope. Many people have tried to prepare, Poirier is quick to acknowledge, but he's not sure Canada's capital has done everything it can to get ready for a big earthquake. For instance, the federal government could lose many of its buildings and need to relocate. "No one's ever talked to me about clearing Bank Street so they can get to the airport," he said. "People would rather pay for the reconstruction than pay for the prevention, politically."

Ottawa isn't the only city subject to the Western Quebec Seismic Zone. In 1732 a relatively big quake shook what was then the small colonial outpost of Montréal. Written descriptions from the time suggest the shaking was severe in some locations and extreme in others, registering as either intensity 9 or 10 on the Modified Mercalli scale. The Geological Survey of Canada estimates the convulsion may have been as powerful as magnitude 6. All over Montréal, chimneys and walls in masonry buildings suffered heavy damage. Much of what we know of the event was recorded by Sister Marie-Anne-Véronique Cuillerier. The fifty-two-year-old nun was the secretary of the order of the Religious Hospitallers of St. Joseph, which was in charge of the Hôtel-Dieu hospital. In frequent and dramatic dispatches to the religious houses of France, she described the difficulties of life in New France, from the bombardments of British ships to "clouds of caterpillars sent by the Lord's justice." Of the earthquake, she wrote: "It was on 16 September, at a quarter past eleven, that the first tremor was heard and felt." It knocked down 567 chimneys, made people run outside in panic, and cracked the walls of nearly all the houses. "Nothing can be more terrible than to see church towers and houses bending like reeds and swaying as badly as if they had been made of cards," Sister Cuillerier wrote. She asked for funds to assist with rebuilding.

Her account also makes it clear that Montréal suffered through a long series of aftershocks, which prompted many people to stay outdoors rather than risk sleeping inside: "Public prayers did not move the Lord to pity, who was content to keep His whole people in a constant state of alarm for more than nine months." One particular aftershock was so large it rivalled the initial earthquake: "God revenged Himself on the night of 25-26 October and caused a tremor like the first one to be heard." Though Sister Cuillerier made no mention of any deaths, a later report did. A decade later, Reverend Matthias Plant submitted a report about earthquakes in New England to the Royal Society of London, claiming the 1732 Montréal earthquake "did damage to one hundred and eighty-five houses [and] killed seven persons."

The Western Quebec Seismic Zone has produced other memorable events. In 1944, the day after Labour Day, thousands of people in the border town of Cornwall, Ontario, 120 kilometres southwest of Montréal, were jolted out of bed in the middle of the night.

"There was an awful roar which sounded as though hell had opened up and let loose," Constable Eddie Firn told the Associated Press. "Women were fainting all over the place, some of them were crying hysterically." The article made no mention of how local men reacted, but it did report local phone lines were jammed in Cornwall and nearby Massena, New York, as nervous residents phoned police and local newspapers. Thousands of chimneys were damaged on both sides of the border, as were several schools. A brick wall fell through the gymnasium roof at the Cornwall Collegiate and Vocational School. Many houses were deemed uninhabitable and in need of major repairs to masonry, plumbing, and foundations. In St. Lawrence County, New York, many wells completely dried up. (Exactly how earthquakes affect well-water levels isn't known, but it may be that new cracks in the rocks allow water to drop. In other quakes, well-water levels have increased.)

The magnitude-5.8 earthquake remains the largest recorded in New York with modern seismographic instruments, but it claimed no lives and is considered a moderate quake. With both Canada and the United States more concerned with the Second World War, many newspapers ignored the Cornwall–Massena earthquake altogether. Others buried it under updates on the US Pacific Fleet's fiery air war against the Japanese or the Canadian Army chasing the Nazis north into Italy. But the Associated Press quoted Harvard University seismologist L. Don Leet's suggestion that "cities take precautions because of an increasing frequency of quakes." Leet noted the earthquake followed another centred in Ossipee, New Hampshire, four years earlier, arguing that quakes in the area were becoming more frequent and warning that if the epicentre had been near a large city like Boston, "it would have constituted a real hazard." It would "only be prudent" for cities to prepare, especially for the fires that were likely to follow. His point that a moderate quake is only a serious concern if it happens near a big city is fair, but city officials in Boston and Montréal should remember their cities are within reach of the Western Quebec Seismic Zone and the neighbouring Charlevoix Seismic Zone, and that both zones might produce even bigger earthquakes.

The 1925 Charlevoix–Kamouraska quake rumbled out of the St. Lawrence River valley, about one hundred kilometres north of Quebec City. The jarring headline across the top of the Quebec City daily *Le Soleil* screamed "UN VIOLENT TREMBLEMENT DE TERRE"—a violent earthquake. The shaking lasted twenty-five seconds and was felt from Atlantic Canada to Lake Ontario. The 1925 quake is now considered to have been a magnitude-6.2 event, and the big fear today is that a similar-size quake might strike closer to Quebec City or Montréal. The *really* big fear is that an even bigger quake will shake the area, and unfortunately for residents, it's happened before. In 1663, not far from the epicentre of the 1925 quake, the ground under the St. Lawrence River trembled even more violently. The quake was centred somewhere between the Malbaie River, on the north shore of the St. Lawrence, and the Ouelle River on the south. About three thousand French colonists were living in the vicinity along with bigger populations of Algonquin and Iroquois.

Father Jérôme Lalemant, the head of the Jesuit Missionaries in Quebec, wrote a vivid account to his superiors in Rome:

> On the fifth of February, 1663, towards half past five in the evening, a loud roaring was heard at the same time throughout the length and breadth of the Canadas. The noise, which gave the impression that the house was on fire, made all rush outdoors to escape so unexpected a conflagration; but instead of smoke and flames, people were much surprised to behold the Walls tottering and all the stones in motion, as if they had been detached. Roofs seemed to bend down in one direction, and then back again in the other, Bells rang of their own accord;

beams, joists, and boards creaked; and the earth leaped up, and made the palisade stakes dance in a way that would have seemed incredible, had we not witnessed it in different places.

Then all left their houses, animals took flight, children cried in the streets, and men and women, seized with terror, knew not where to take refuge, — expecting every moment to be either overwhelmed under the ruins of the houses, or swallowed up in to some abyss that was to open beneath their feet.

Father Lalemant also shared a telling detail for modern scientists, describing the long, nausea-inducing waves that often accompany significant quakes and likening it to "the same heaving of the stomach that one suffers on the water." Father Charles Simon of Trois-Rivières used similar language. "The earth was shaken with so great a force that it leaped up to the height of a foot," he recorded, "and rolled in the manner of a skiff tossed by the waves."

The quake caused serious landslides. Large wooded slopes crashed through river ice that was two metres thick. Other hillsides were shaken loose and left more vulnerable to future slides, like the one that destroyed part of the town of Saint-Jean-Vianney in 1971. A long rain storm and unusually snowy winter triggered the event, but geologists believe the 1663 earthquake created the conditions that made a large landslide possible more than three hundred years later. Forty homes built above the slide were dragged down along with the slope, and thirty-one people were killed.

In 2011 John Ebel at Boston College's Weston Observatory conducted a new analysis of the 1663 Charlevoix earthquake and concluded it had been a monster; possibly as powerful as magnitude 7.8 and no smaller than magnitude 6.9. He based his findings on historical reports of the intensity of shaking and damage to chimneys and other masonry as far away as Boston. Ebel believes the Charlevoix earthquake was comparable to the 1811 and 1812 earthquakes in New Madrid, Missouri. Other scientists doubt the region can produce such large quakes and believe the 1663 quake was no larger than magnitude 7. But a future earthquake of that size would still inflict serious damage on the closest major city: Quebec City.

Quebec City is more than four hundred years old, and the metropolitan area is home to more than eight hundred thousand people. Its historic old town, so popular with tourists and home to roughly sixty thousand people, is the greatest concern. Old Quebec is a UNESCO World Heritage Site, deemed "one of the best examples of a fortified colonial city." Its stone ramparts, bastions, churches, convents, citadel, Château Frontenac hotel, and narrow streets are alive with history. But engineering assessments predict that strong shaking could damage more than nine thousand old masonry and wood buildings in Quebec City, and leave 1,100 damaged beyond repair.

Roughly eight million people now live in the busy corridor between Quebec City and Ottawa, and the region constitutes a significant seismic concern, both because of historic earthquakes and the fact that so many buildings were built without taking seismic risk into account. The region has had a few modest shakers, however, that have jostled some of the population out of complacency. Before the 2010 Ottawa quake, Quebec was rattled by a magnitude-5.9 quake in 1988 that caused a few heart attacks and damaged brick buildings, including the Montréal East City Hall, an old unreinforced masonry building that stood on seventeen metres of clay. It was so seriously damaged it was torn down.

Its loss left local officials wondering about 1,500 other civic structures and how an earthquake would damage them. The City of Montréal has been quietly assessing them to identify which ones are most at risk. The charming cobblestone streets and brittle old buildings of Vieux-Montréal are an obvious concern, but Marie-José Nollet, a professor of engineering at Université du Québec à

Montréal, notes the city has many more vulnerable structures in its old industrial areas, including brick warehouses and early concrete-frame buildings with no shear walls and little reinforcement. Nollet lacks good records of which buildings have received seismic reinforcement in the past, something that makes risk assessment difficult.

The natural hazard may be lower in Montréal than it is on the West Coast, but the risk of loss of human life and property is still a real concern. Montréal is Canada's second-largest city, boasting a population of four million. Many of its highway overpasses have been coming apart in bits and pieces for decades, and some have failed even without an earthquake. In 2006, a twenty-metre stretch of the De la Concorde overpass collapsed in the suburb of Laval, crushing two cars and killing five people. Many overpasses have been repaired or replaced since then, and yet a lot of aging infrastructure remains.

The type of earthquake determines the degree of risk. If a local fault rumbles close to Montréal, high-frequency shaking could devastate old unreinforced brick buildings. Other buildings that withstand sudden shocks might be at higher risk from more distant earthquakes, because unconsolidated sediments and filled land can amplify the longer-frequency seismic waves. Like Charleston, Montréal could lose otherwise robust buildings in its old port area, because the ground beneath them simply can't take the shake. For the region as a whole, Natural Resources Canada pegs the risk of a damaging, potentially deadly earthquake hitting Montréal, Ottawa, or Quebec City at anywhere from 5 to 15 percent in the next fifty years. In 2017 the insurance company Swiss Re forecast the cost of a repeat of the 1732 quake at more than $45 billion.

Some people will interpret cataclysmic forecasts from insurers as the pressure tactics of an industry that's keen to sell more policies and secure financial assurances from governments at the same time. Indeed, we should probably view predictions of future calamity with some skepticism, as precise estimates of death or financial loss are exceedingly difficult to make. But we shouldn't forget the disasters that have already taken place. Between 1994 and 2013, earthquakes and tsunamis around the world killed 750,000 people. That's more than the deaths from hurricanes, cyclones, floods, drought, wildfires, and several other natural disasters combined.

Fortunately, there is evidence that changing attitudes are leading to more preparation and more innovation. A year after the 2010 earthquake sent politicians scrambling outdoors in Ottawa, the West Block of Parliament Hill closed for a seven-year major renovation and seismic retrofit. After the West Block reopened, politicians and staff moved into temporary accommodation so that Centre Block could be closed for similar improvements. Other government buildings in the area are also scheduled for upgrades, including the eighty-year-old Supreme Court of Canada, which will receive a steel-frame reinforcement. The project will cost Canadian taxpayers billions of dollars (the final cost won't be known until it's done), but the hope is that the renovations, coupled with the fact that Parliament is built on bedrock, will keep the central buildings of government standing and fully functional immediately after a strong earthquake.

While governments may be able to afford expensive seismic repairs, many private property owners will decide the work is simply too expensive. But an innovation being developed at the University of Ottawa holds the promise of less disruptive and possibly cheaper fixes. Civil engineer and professor Murat Saatcioglu is working on a newer method of retrofitting old brick walls. He and his team of researchers have developed a material called fibre-reinforced polymer, which resembles wallpaper but is made of a durable carbon fibre. It's thin enough that it can wrap around almost anything, including brick walls, but when it's mixed with an epoxy resin, it becomes incredibly strong. Aircraft manufacturers such as Airbus have used it to make wing flaps. When old brick walls are covered in fibre-reinforced polymer, and that shield extends well down into the foundation, the building is both stronger and more flexible.

Saatcioglu and his team have built large unreinforced masonry walls on top of an earthquake simulator, covered the walls in fibre-reinforced polymer, and simulated an earthquake. The results of their tests suggest brick walls reinforced with this lightweight covering are more robust than those without. Other vulnerable structures can be made more earthquake resistant, like old bridge columns that are wrapped with stiff steel wire, making them less likely to explode under extreme stress. The concrete columns of taller towers can also be wrapped to make them less likely to collapse. Saatcioglu acknowledges none of these fixes are easy, and at roughly $400 per square metre, they're not cheap. But that's less expensive than many traditional fixes, and innovations like these give owners more options to make their buildings safer — "not as many as one would like to see," he admits. "But it's coming. Very slowly, it's coming."

There are other important seismic safety improvements coming to Ontario and Quebec in the years ahead. The Geological Survey of Canada has been developing an earthquake early-warning system that will be able to send emergency alerts to millions of people's cell phones, as well as key public buildings and infrastructure, seconds before the ground starts shaking. The network is starting in British Columbia, but seismologist Alison Bird says "we're going to be extending the network around the Ottawa River valley and the St. Lawrence Seaway because that's also a high-risk area." Bird expects it will be finished by 2024.

For some, though, the pace of seismic change in Ontario and Quebec is too slow. Christie Rowe is a geology professor at McGill University. A native of California, she lived through frightening earthquakes long before she studied them. "One of my most salient memories was of the 1989 Loma Prieta," she recalls. "I was eleven, and I'd just got home from swim practice when it struck."

Rowe waited anxiously for hours, wondering if her father, who was commuting from San Francisco to their home north of the city, was crushed under one of the bridges that collapsed. Keenly aware of what earthquakes can do to cities, Rowe knows the seismic hazards in and around Montréal are real. She recognizes the occasional magnitude-3 quake when it rumbles under the city, and she also sees many of her neighbours dismiss the rumbles as nothing more than a passing truck. When asked if awareness of the earthquake risk in Montréal is adequate, Rowe is blunt: "It's not addressed in the schools, and it's definitely not something that's emphasized in society at large."

Rowe is reluctant to specify the risk in Quebec because scientists don't know the full extent of natural hazards in the region. They have identified a number of faults and have evidence of past earthquakes, but there are likely many more potentially active faults that they have not yet mapped. As in much of the eastern United States, seismic information in and around Quebec is lacking. The frustration in Rowe's voice is evident as she describes what she calls the "lack-of-data circular hole" that she and other scientists must navigate. "It's hard to argue a risk until you've established what the record is," she says, "and you don't know about the record until you go look, and you can't get the money to go look until you can argue there's a risk!"

And yet Rowe and ten colleagues across Canada have high hopes that they'll be able to change things. In 2020 they made an ambitious proposal to the National Sciences and Engineering Research Council to establish a new earthquake science research program that will train as many as sixty graduate students across the country in disciplines from fault geology to seismology to landslides to tsunamis. "We need to produce more highly competent, multi-disciplinary scientists," Rowe insists, "and we need them yesterday."

Chapter 12

THE UNFATHOMED ATLANTIC

While tsunamis are more common in the Pacific Ocean, a tragedy on Newfoundland's Burin Peninsula is a deadly reminder that the Atlantic can also be lethal to coastal communities. A quake in 1929 triggered a geological chain of events that proved fatal to the residents of tiny Newfoundland fishing villages.

The winter's first snow had started falling on Halifax, Nova Scotia, sometime in the afternoon of Monday, November 19, 1929. The wind built into a gale as the sun began to sink into the western horizon. Twelve minutes before it set, the ground under the city started trembling. Panicked people rushed outside; three people in Simpson's department store fainted. The shaking triggered vivid memories of the 1917 Halifax Explosion, which flattened the waterfront, killing two thousand and injuring nine thousand more.

The earthquake that shook Halifax on this autumn day spared the city's residents, but it created plenty of drama in Cape Breton, and people assessed the damage, which included rock slides, toppled chimneys, and several collapsed barns near Sydney. In the theatre, a scene shifter fell seven metres to the stage floor; in the courthouse, a witness on the stand fainted. As the wind blew stronger and the snow turned to rain, people along the Cape Breton coast noticed rising water and minor flooding. The *Halifax Chronicle* reported the shaking lasted for two minutes in total and included two especially pronounced tremors at 4:33 and 4:35 p.m. The ground force threw the needle of the seismograph at Dalhousie University completely out of position, preventing a full measurement of the peak shaking, but other readings and reports later led scientists to declare the undersea Grand Banks earthquake a magnitude-7.2.

The offshore earthquake triggered a submarine landslide. A giant patch of the Laurentian Slope slid down the steeply slanting ocean floor, all the way down to the Sohm Abyssal Plain, roughly five thousand metres below the surface. The slide of staggering proportions lasted more than twenty hours and severed twelve transatlantic cables in twenty-eight different places. Roughly two hundred cubic kilometres of sediment reached speeds of roughly one hundred kilometres an hour before settling on a patch of ocean floor that was roughly 150,000 kilometres square, significantly larger than Newfoundland. The slide also displaced a colossal volume of water, generating tsunamis that raced out in different directions. The faster wave, recorded on tidal gauges as far south as Charleston, sped through the deeper waters to the east and south at roughly six hundred kilometres an hour and caused minor damage in Bermuda. The other massive tsunami, heading in the opposite direction, would be lethal.

The deadly wave plowed through the much shallower sea towards Newfoundland at about one hundred kilometres an hour. Two and a half hours after the earthquake, at about 7:30 p.m. local time, the first of three tsunami surges struck the Burin Peninsula, some 265 kilometres north of the earthquake epicentre. People who lived in Newfoundland's south coast fishing villages noticed the ocean had withdrawn. They could see ocean floor that normally was never visible. Then they watched the water return in three shocking surges as foaming, breaking waves rose between three and eight metres high along most stretches of the coastline and up to fourteen metres at the heads of some long, narrow bays. In some places the water took as long as ten minutes to reach its peak, giving some fortunate people time to escape to high ground. But for others the deluge was fast and deadly.

The waves lifted houses off their foundations, tore boats from their moorings, and smashed into wharves and fish stores, pulling 280,000 pounds of salt cod back into the ocean. Those who couldn't avoid the first wave were caught up in the dangerous waters. In Stepaside, on Burin Island, the water swept a house with ten people inside fifteen metres out and then back in again. They scrambled out, carrying a man confined to his bed, before the water lifted and crushed the house. Several other houses had similar experiences. Men plunged into the water to break windows and rescue trapped women and children. "Many men were cut severely in such rescue work," the United Press reported, "one man nearly bleeding to death from a severed artery before he could be taken to a physician seven miles distant."

One house floated away as a woman clutching a baby rushed from one lamplit window to another, screaming to the men on shore to save them. Rescuers spent an hour trying to reach a man trapped on his roof but could not save him before the water swept his house away. In the village of Port Au Bras, a father carrying his young children escaped the surging waters through a window, his wife clinging to his shoulders. He made it ashore with his children, but his wife could not hang on and was swept out to sea. A fisherman was able to grab her and bring her closer to the shore, where other rescuers pulled her to safety—but he fell back into the water and drowned moments later. A faithful Newfoundland dog in Port Au Bras "plunged into the receding wave as it carried away the dwelling in which his master and his master's baby girl were trapped," the press reported. "The dog soon was sighted swimming back to shore, the child held high above the water. Waiting hands helped the dog and his human cargo to shore, where the child was received. But the dog escaped from restraining hands and plunged back into the sea.

Nearing the floating dwelling, the dog was caught and crushed in the collapse of another building floating on the surface. His master also perished."

In the village of Lord's Cove, the water swept the two-storey house belonging to the Rennie family off its footings and grounded it in a pond near the beach. Sarah Rennie was at home with her four youngest children at the time; her husband and their two older sons were playing cards at a neighbour's house. After the tsunami, local men rowed out to the house. Sarah and three of her children had drowned in the kitchen. On the second floor, three-year-old Margaret was alive in her crib. "When they got me I was unconscious from the mud and water and everything else," she said seventy-six years later. "They took me and put me down in a big tub of warm water." The tsunami killed twenty-five people on Newfoundland's south coast that night; three later died of injuries they'd received.

The survivors faced a long night ahead on their own. They could not call for help. Though some of the villagers had telephones, none were capable of long-distance communication, and a storm a few days earlier had severed the single telegraph wire that reached St. John's, Newfoundland's capital. No road connected the peninsula to Newfoundland's urban communities. Most of the boats had been swept out to sea. Of the vessels not lost or wrecked, only one had an operating wireless radio, but no one at hand knew how to operate it.

Though the people of the Burin Peninsula could not call out for help, they could tune in to radio signals from the outside world. A few dazed villagers turned on their radios, hoping they might hear news about what had happened. Instead they heard only dance music and songs from remote American cities that were completely oblivious to the tragedy that had just taken place.

When daylight returned on Tuesday, it revealed that whole villages had washed away. The water had dumped some bodies on the shore, tangled in seaweed or fishing nets or both. In Port Au Bras a woman's body was found floating with her dead child clutched in her arms. The drowned corpses of another mother and child were found still inside their house, drifting eight kilometres offshore, a lamp burning on a table in an upstairs bedroom.

The news of what had happened made it to other ports and to St. John's three days later, when the SS *Portia* stopped at Burin harbour and sent a radio message for help. When the first ships arrived, their crews found survivors traumatized. In Port au Bras, Ern Cheeseman tried to steady his shaking hand to write his brother a letter about the ordeal. "Excuse this scribble but we are not over the shock yet," he wrote. "You could hear the poor humans who were caught, screaming, women and men praying out loud. Oh God, Jack, it was terrible."

At first, the disaster was called, incorrectly, a tidal wave. It wasn't until the 1950s that scientists understood the basic geological cause and effect of how a quake triggered the undersea landslide that in turn triggered the tsunami. Outside the scientific community, and possibly Newfoundland, it's arguable that most people along the East Coast didn't take tsunamis seriously until they saw the footage of the Indian Ocean tsunami in 2004 and the Japanese tsunami in 2011. Now, most people are at least vaguely aware of the devastation the ocean can unleash, but what's not so well understood is exactly where and how frequently tsunamis strike the East Coast.

The good news is that there is no subduction zone along the North American Atlantic coast, and earthquakes large enough to trigger tsunamis themselves, typically magnitude 7 and up, are rare. Only a handful of really big earthquakes in the region have come close: Charlevoix in 1663, Cape Ann in 1755, Charleston in 1886, the 1929 quake near Newfoundland, and a magnitude 7.3 under Baffin Bay in the Arctic in 1933. But not all of these produced deadly tsunamis. While the Cascadia Subduction Zone at least offers a rough timeline of how frequently it produces tsunamis, the timeline on the East Coast is less clear.

Scientists have been trying to change that. In 2009 the National Oceanic and Atmospheric Administration surveyed a 1,200-kilometre stretch of ocean floor off the Atlantic coast. This important bathymetric data helps scientists make more accurate maps of submarine canyons and learn more about past landslides along the ocean floor. The data that NOAA gathered suggests the largest landslides along the east coast of the United States have occurred along the southern New England continental slope.

The possibility of an East Coast tsunami generated a lot more attention in 2012, after a swarm of small offshore earthquakes occurred about 270 kilometres east of Boston. None of them were anywhere near the magnitude of a quake that could trigger a tsunami on its own, but the possibility that a moderate undersea quake could strike in just the right — or wrong — spot and trigger another massive submarine landslide troubled some scientists. The tectonic setting responsible for that swarm of quakes, seismologist John Ebel notes, is similar to the location of the 1929 slide that triggered the tsunami in Newfoundland. "Geologically, it looks the same. The earthquakes are occurring right at the edge of the continental shelf."

The probability of a major tsunami striking a large East Coast city remains unclear. While American scientists have gathered useful bathymetric data along the coast, tsunami calculations rely on more than just local information. As both the Pacific Ocean and Indian Ocean have demonstrated, tsunamis can be deadly thousands of kilometres away from the seismic events that trigger them. The 2004 Indian Ocean tsunami killed people ten thousand kilometres away in South Africa, the 1964 Alaska earthquake tsunami killed people five thousand kilometres to the south in Los Angeles, and the 1960 Chilean subduction monster triggered a tsunami that drowned people in Japan, some seventeen thousand kilometres away from the quake's epicentre.

The National Tsunami Hazard Mitigation Program has identified three possible sources of long-distance tsunamis that could conceivably strike the East Coast. The closest comes from the deep waters of the Puerto Rico Trench, where the sea floor is more than eight thousand metres beneath the surface. In contrast to the deep trenches of the Pacific Ocean, the Puerto Rico Trench lies along a boundary that doesn't subduct. In other words, the two plates that come together in the Puerto Rico Trench are mostly sliding past each other, instead of one sinking beneath the other. The geology of the region is not well understood, but what is known is that it can create big earthquakes, including a magnitude-8.1 temblor north of Hispaniola in 1946 that triggered a tsunami that killed about 1,600 people. The sea flooded into the towns of Puerto Plata and Mantanzas, on the north coast of the Dominican Republic, minutes after the devastating quake. In some cases, the quake trapped victims and the waves drowned them, like a group of around forty men and boys in Mantanzas who'd been standing under a metal roof watching a cock fight. The roof collapsed, and the tsunami washed over them soon after.

To be clear, the greatest tsunami risk from the Puerto Rico Trench is to Puerto Rico itself and the surrounding Caribbean islands. In 1918 a magnitude-7.5 earthquake fifteen kilometres off Puerto Rico's northwest coast killed seventy-six people and triggered a tsunami that washed ashore less than ten minutes after the quake, killing forty more. In some low-lying areas of Puerto Rico's west coast the water rose more than five metres. A draft US Geological Survey hazard map gives the city of Mayagüez roughly the same probability of a damaging earthquake as Seattle.

The risk in the Caribbean is relatively clear. It remains to be seen whether or not the Puerto Rico Trench could trigger a large submarine landslide that then triggers a tsunami big enough to reach the mainland United States. The trench faces north and east into the Atlantic Ocean, without much land that would prevent large tsunami waves from sweeping out in those directions. The direction of the waves would depend on a number of factors, including where along the trench an earthquake or slide occurred. In 2012 the Geological Survey of Canada said the northeast Caribbean "may present a significant tsunami threat, but the potential hazard is poorly understood, requiring much further study." Scientists, fortunately, are taking the risk more seriously than they once did, according to Christa van Hillebrandt-Andrade, a manager with NOAA's Caribbean Tsunami Warning Program. "Before 2004, we thought an earthquake of about 8.0 was about right for the largest we might see in the Caribbean, based on the history of earthquakes there and the length and motion of the faults," she told *Science Daily*. "But now some think that several faults in the region could be capable of producing earthquakes of 8.6."

The second possible threat comes from a fault zone on the other side of the Atlantic. The Azores–Gibraltar transform fault stretches from the Strait of Gibraltar out to the Azores Triple Junction, where the North American plate, the Eurasian plate, and the African plate meet under the ocean. The transform fault's resumé includes the devastating Great Lisbon Earthquake and a tsunami believed to have reached Bonavista, Newfoundland, in 1755. Some scientists think the risk that the Azores–Gibraltar fault will claim any lives in North America in the future is low. Computer models suggest undersea mountains west of Portugal will likely slow and disrupt any giant waves headed for the coast. But, as is the case with so many other potential ocean hazards, they might have a better idea if they had more data from the ocean floor.

The third and final threat of distant tsunamis is the most frightening—and the most contentious among scientists. The volcanic island of La Palma in the Canary Islands represents a serious concern for some geologists. Simon Day of University College London and Steven Ward of the University of California–Santa Cruz have studied whether an eruption of the volcano Cumbre Vieja could trigger another disaster elsewhere. The specific concern is a giant crack that appeared during an eruption in 1949, causing the western flank of the volcano to slip down a few metres. The volcano is now quiet, but the two geologists wonder if the giant five-hundred-cubic-kilometre flank might collapse the next time the volcano erupts, unleashing what some scientists call a megatsunami. The section of rock is colossal, measuring somewhere between fifteen and twenty kilometres in length and roughly the same in width. The fear is that this enormous section could one day plunge into the ocean, creating a wave bigger than any ever witnessed, a "rare geological time bomb," as a BBC documentary described it. The terrifying—and for now hypothetical—megatsunami could sweep five thousand kilometres across the Atlantic Ocean, striking Boston first and then wreaking havoc up and down the coast. Even those concerned about a megatsunami say there's little to worry about as long as the volcano isn't rumbling, and other scientists believe it's unlikely that the western flank of the volcano would crash into the ocean all at once. George Pararas-Carayannis, an oceanographer and the former director of the International Tsunami Information Center, argues the threat from the collapse of volcanoes, like Cumbre Vieja in the Canaries and Kilauea in Hawaii, is "greatly overstated." As of 2019, the National Tsunami Hazard Mitigation Program rates the tsunami hazard to the Atlantic coast as "low to very low."

Maybe East Coasters shouldn't panic, but does that mean they should ignore the risk? Scientists say the answer is twofold and relatively simple: prepare for the worst, and continue the research. This could sound self-serving. After all, the scientific community will benefit first and foremost from an influx of investment in new research. But in the long run, all vulnerable communities will benefit from more information. After all, the 2010 Christchurch quake rumbled out of a fault that geologists didn't know existed.

A team of researchers at the Geological Survey of Canada recently discovered a previously unknown risk on the Atlantic coast. They looked for evidence of other historical submarine landslides on the

Scotian Slope, where the 1929 Grand Banks earthquake and tsunami originated. Scientists had long estimated the slope produced massive slides only once every ten thousand years or so, but they'd done little research. This team collected core samples from the ocean floor, and what they found suggests that large submarine slides, like the one that caused the 1929 tsunami, happen about once every thousand years. They based that rough calculation on evidence of the 1929 event and three similar slides in the last four thousand years. This is a significant discovery, but what exactly does it mean for people who live along the coast?

"Of course you tell the public that it's once every thousand years instead of once every ten thousand years, and most people's eyes glaze over," marine geoscientist Calvin Campbell, at the Geological Survey of Canada, says. "They just think, I'm not going to lose too much sleep over that." Campbell is quick to acknowledge that it's still not clear how many of these past slides triggered tsunamis. "I always tell people that it would be foolish for us to ignore it, because it happened relatively recently. Geologically speaking, it happened yesterday."

Campbell and his fellow scientists recommend "a re-evaluation of submarine landslide risk across the western North Atlantic margin." That requires more data: more sea-floor mapping, more analysis of historic undersea slides, more slope stability analysis, and more numerical modelling of tsunami potential. This is true in the United States, but it's especially true north of the border. "Canada is lagging every other developed country in terms of the amount of offshore bathymetric mapping we're doing," Campbell warns. "There's huge areas of the offshore that haven't been mapped in high resolution, definitely on the East Coast."

Canadians might think their country can't afford this level of research. The United States has a much bigger population than Canada and a lot more taxpayers to foot the bill. But Campbell points out that Australia, with a similar population density to Canada, has mapped its entire coastline to modern standards. Tsunamis in recent decades have demonstrated how the specific characteristics of local seabeds affect their size and force. "And that could be researched quite easily," Campbell said. "You could quite quickly get an idea of what were some areas that needed to have resiliency built into them."

Tsunamis can do more damage than the earthquakes that trigger them, but we know more about the land under our feet than the floor under the waves. The data discrepancy between land and sea is especially concerning right along the coast. The Point Lepreau Nuclear Generating Station on the New Brunswick side of the Bay of Fundy is a good example. In a licence-renewal hearing in 2017, the Canadian Nuclear Safety Commission considered all sorts of hazards that could conceivably cause trouble at Canada's only nuclear plant on an ocean coastline, from meteor strikes to plane crashes to dam failures. Earthquake and tsunami hazards were also taken into account. A moderate earthquake, estimated as magnitude 5.9, shook St. Stephen, centred about ninety kilometres down the coast and at the border with Maine, in 1904. The nuclear facility is built only fourteen metres above the Bay of Fundy, which, as any New Brunswicker worth their salt will tell you, has the world's highest tides. NB Power, the electric utility that owns Point Lepreau, insists the plant can endure a large earthquake and is high enough to withstand a tsunami. Nuclear critics are skeptical: fourteen metres is roughly the same height as the tsunami wave that crippled the Fukushima Daiichi plant. NB Power argues the Bay of Fundy is more protected than the open coast, because Nova Scotia and Sable Island will act as natural breakwaters and protect the bay from a tsunami's worst effects. But Ronald Babin, a Université de Moncton social scientist and nuclear critic, notes that Japanese nuclear officials believed Fukushima was safe, too.

New Brunswick is hardly among the most seismically active places in the world. But scientists know a lot less about tsunamis in the Atlantic than they do in the Pacific. Communities up and down the Atlantic coast simply don't know the full extent of the tsunami hazard they face.

Chapter 13

COUNTERING COMPLACENCY

While a relatively small number of scientists keep applying for more funding to expand our scientific knowledge of natural hazards, many millions of us pay little or no attention. Of those who do think about natural disasters, most worry more about hurricanes, tornadoes, floods, fires, and climate change than earthquakes and tsunamis. But the clock keeps ticking down to the next big earthquake. If the clock ticks slowly, we will have time to better our geological understanding of some of the areas at risk. Perhaps more of our cities and towns will have adopted stricter building codes and a few might have adopted mandatory retrofit laws. No doubt they'll be made considerably stronger *after* the next really big North American earthquake. What will it take to make them stronger before? This is the key question in cities that will experience damaging earthquakes in the future but haven't had any in living memory.

"One of the reasons for not doing something is not having experienced it," Robert Gifford, an environmental psychologist at the University of Victoria, explains. "It's what we call the crisis-response mentality. You don't put up the sign that there's a dangerous curve on the highway until somebody's already gone off the road, or you don't do earthquake preparation until one has already happened." Many people who have survived major earthquakes notice the lack of concern among those who have not. "I think it's one of those things that until you live through you really don't know what to expect," observes Paula Romagosa, who was six years old when a massive earthquake shook her home country of Ecuador. She remembers it vividly. "I couldn't get out of bed. I could see the wall across from my bed moving, and I could see it cracking, and I was just terrified of that. I couldn't get out of bed until my dad came and just dragged me out." Romagosa wonders if people who haven't experienced the terror firsthand don't realize how serious it is.

Honn Kao, who now works for the Geological Survey of Canada, shares a similar view. In 1999, he returned home to Taiwan two days after a massive magnitude-7.7 earthquake ravaged the island and says no one who lives through a "huge ground shaking" will ever want to repeat the experience. The quake killed two thousand and left another one hundred thousand homeless, but Honn thinks outsiders would be just as surprised by the disaster's long-term impacts. Taiwan's power stations were heavily damaged, and its nuclear reactors shut down automatically, and for many, that led to the loss of water and electricity. Honn and his family had to walk down nine flights to collect two pails of water—and carry them back up—at least three times each day. "The impact goes far beyond just the number of fatalities and injuries. It's all the lives of millions of people who all of a sudden have a change that they do not expect," he says. "These are the kinds of things that you will not be able to imagine unless you actually live through it."

That may explain why some of the best-prepared people have direct experience with disasters. Both Anne Mullens and Claire Kelly lived through big earthquakes in Japan before returning to Canada, though the earthquakes were more than forty years apart. Mullens was ten years old and staying with her family in Tokyo when the city shook in 1968. She remembers hearing a grinding noise like she'd never heard before, followed by a sudden, violent shaking. A goldfish bowl on top of the television rose in the air "in a cartoon-like fashion" and smashed on the floor. Today, at her home in Victoria, Mullens has stockpiled a long list of essentials that includes emergency medical supplies, a propane stove, a tent, money, non-perishable food, and a wrench to turn off the neighbour's gas line. She even has a few chickens that produce three eggs a day. Claire Kelly is just as passionate about being prepared. She lived through the 2011 Tohoku earthquake: "I felt like I was on an amusement ride that I couldn't get off." When she came home she gave everyone in her family an emergency kit for Christmas. Kelly now lives in New Brunswick, but she hasn't forgotten what she learned in Japan. "To this day I make sure my gas tank is full and my phone is fully charged," she says.

In 1985 reporter Deborah Wilson endured the giant earthquake that brought Mexico City to its knees. She'd just taken a job in the city and was staying in a friend's fourth-floor apartment when she awoke to the violent shaking of the magnitude-8 quake. It felt, she remembers, "like being in a boat on a sea of concrete." After the shaking, she saw a nearby building collapse and spent days reporting on the tragic destruction of the city. Her experience in Mexico compelled her to research and report the risk to Vancouver and Victoria. "In our lifetime or our children's or our grandchildren's lifetime, there will be a similar earthquake here," she says.

Firsthand experience isn't the only factor that determines who prepares and to what extent. Helene Joffe, a professor of psychology at University College London, and a team of researchers at the university's EPICentre for Natural Hazards Resilience, have studied attitudes towards earthquake preparation in several countries. They've found most people living in seismic zones generally do little or nothing to prepare for earthquakes. One study compared attitudes in the United States, Turkey, and Japan, focusing on cities that will have damaging earthquakes but have not had any big ones recently: Seattle, Izmir, and Osaka. Millions of people in these cities are not prepared for an earthquake, despite the significant risk of a major event in all three. Joffe attributes that to anxiety, fatalism, and a distrust of local authorities.

No doubt some degree of anxiety sparks many of the precautions we take, from seatbelts to smoke detectors. But anxiety can also paralyze people into doing nothing. Fatalism — "the belief that people cannot change the way events will happen and that events, especially bad ones, cannot be avoided" — according to the Cambridge English Dictionary — also leads some people to do nothing. Of course others will avoid making preparations because they have faith that a higher power will protect them. Either way the end result is the same: they do not take measures to stay alive during and after an earthquake.

Distrust of local authorities, meanwhile, is understandable in countries where corruption is common and laws are routinely ignored. Helene Joffe found distrust barely factored in the United States or Japan, but it was a huge factor in Turkey. Turkish media and government reports often state that three-quarters of the buildings in the country lack the design documents and permits that were required for construction. Many of these buildings went up with little or no supervision and inspection. As a result, many Turkish buildings contain crumbling concrete, rusting steel reinforcements, and other critical weaknesses that could contribute to collapse in an earthquake. In 1999, the magnitude-7.4 Kocaeli earthquake killed seventeen thousand and left half a million homeless. A year later, Turkish scientists estimated the likelihood of another deadly quake on the North Anatolian fault by 2030 at 62 percent (plus or minus 15 percent).

People in Seattle seem to have done more to prepare than their Japanese or Turkish counterparts. Helene Joffe ascribes this to American individualism, in contrast to Japan's "cultural and political emphasis on collectivism and state action." She speculates that "cultural processes that direct responsibility for earthquake protection away from oneself and towards other agents might undermine individual preparations in both Japan and Turkey. It gets left to government." Robert Gifford at the University of Victoria tells people that relying on government is a mistake. "In general governments don't respond by supplying everything that you've lost, and neither does insurance," he points out. Personal preparations pay off after the disaster, he says, and they ease anxiety beforehand. "We call it perceived control, thinking that you're able to do something about it."

Yet many of us do nothing, and for myriad reasons. Gifford calls them the Dragons of Inaction. They include social pressure not to complain or do anything, a feeling that preparing is too difficult or too expensive, confidence that a few supplies set aside in the basement will be enough, and what psychologists call temporal dislocation, which allows someone to shrug off the threat of disaster as something unlikely to happen in their lifetime. How can emergency planners slay the Dragons of Inaction? Gifford thinks the key is to convince people and communities that their actions can make a difference. "I think it comes down to raising awareness of the possibility, but pairing it with the sense that you are able to do something about it."

Talk on the West Coast about mandating seismic retrofits is abundant, but moving from talk to action can be exceedingly difficult. That has certainly been the case in Portland, Oregon, where city commissioners tried in 2018 to tackle that long list of 1,600 vulnerable brick buildings. They debated a new mandate that would require the building owners to perform retrofits within ten or fifteen years. Some viewed this as a simple and sensible solution but many owners complained. It is especially expensive to fortify these buildings properly. Many old brick beauties have received half-measures, like removing the parapets and cornices or fastening them to the roof. That should prevent a cascade of bricks from raining down in a moderate earthquake. But those buildings

THREE — The East Coast

also need the more expensive work of bolting floors to walls, and without it they remain extremely vulnerable to collapse in a major earthquake.

Building owners argued for more time and only the minimum level of seismic retrofit. Some urged commissioners to abandon the idea completely, arguing a combination of market forces and natural forces would take care of the situation—eventually. "When or if the earthquake happens," the Hawthorne Boulevard Business Association argued, "then the properties can be sold and new buildings will rise out of the rubble." The business association said nothing about the many dead bodies that may have to be pulled out of the rubble first.

Owners should not necessarily be dismissed as preoccupied with their money. Expensive repairs could affect many low-income renters, who might face significant rent increases or even lose their homes to demolition if their landlords can't afford the repair bills. Pippa Arend lives in one of twelve units in a 109-year-old brick building that she also owns. She told the *Portland Mercury* the necessary upgrades to her building will cost close to $2 million. "I would be economically forced into a state of blight," she says, "or my building comes down and becomes condos."

In many big cities with high housing costs and growing homeless populations, an obvious safety measure quickly turns into a social-justice dilemma for local politicians. Eric Holdeman, the veteran emergency planner in Seattle, bristles at the suggestion that poor people will be hurt by mandatory retrofits. "If you look at who disaster impacts, it always impacts the poor, low-income people more because they're in substandard housing," he notes. "We're just setting them up to be the victims again." The people who have opposed mandatory seismic retrofit measures in both Portland and Seattle have put historical preservation and affordable housing on the same level as life safety, he argues. "They're all being treated as equal, and life safety is not equal to me. I think you've got to put a line in the sand and get it done and have it done." Cities like Los Angeles have started setting mandatory requirements for seismic assessments and retrofits, and even Vancouver, which has done comparatively little to compel property owners to make buildings safe, has recently started taking a closer look at its towers. Many people presume governments have always been proactive about the safety of public structures. But the truth is that many municipal, state or provincial, and federal governments are delaying these crucial, life-saving steps, and some aren't even considering them. In other words, many of our governments are complacent. It might even be argued that our building code is complacent, too.

"One of the really big issues," civil engineer Perry Adebar says, "is that people think the building code is something that ensures buildings do really well. And it's not. It's a useful document, and engineers have to follow it, but it's full of holes." One of the biggest problems with most building codes, he argues, is that no one is really certain of their ultimate purpose. "Are we just trying to make sure people don't die in the earthquake or do we want buildings to be usable? And that's a big debate that's going on worldwide."

The design of any new building includes a lot of things that have nothing to do with safety. The City of Vancouver made aesthetics mandatory, declaring that "higher buildings must establish a significant and recognizable new benchmark for architectural creativity and excellence, while making a significant contribution to the beauty and visual power of the city's skyline." But Adebar says the city failed to make seismic resilience of buildings an explicit requirement for many years "because of a mistaken belief that the Canadian building code ensures that buildings will perform adequately during an earthquake." The fact that the building code requires buildings to remain standing during an earthquake, but not necessarily usable after the quake, puts the post-quake future of many modern buildings in doubt.

But policies can change, and so can people. In Seaside, Oregon, long-time school superintendent Doug Dougherty has thought a lot about how to overcome complacency and convince reluctant communities to prepare for the worst. Over the years, as he campaigned to close vulnerable schools, he encountered much resistance. Some people would simply avoid the topic with him, others didn't believe something so awful could happen in the place they'd lived their whole lives, and still others recognized the danger but didn't want to talk about it. "The comment I heard over and over again was, 'It just makes us look stupid for living here.' And they don't want to be reminded of that."

But Dougherty kept reminding the people of Seaside that one day one of nature's most terrifying forces would wash over their homes. Slowly, year by year, he convinced more and more of his fellow citizens that they could do something about it. When Seaside residents first voted on whether to pay for a new school campus, the proposition failed. But Dougherty learned something from the process. He focused on smaller, more achievable precautions. He introduced the first tsunami evacuation drills and convinced his staff to learn ham radio so they could communicate with emergency officials if all other means of communications failed. Little by little, one person at a time, Dougherty and other like-minded individuals convinced the community to prepare.

That kind of collective approach to preparation is key, according to Will Horter, who witnessed the benefits in West Oakland during the 1989 Loma Prieta quake. "It takes a community to survive," he's concluded. West Oakland was one of the poorest neighbourhoods he'd ever lived in, but Horter thought it had the best sense of community, which was invaluable after the earthquake. When the power went out and the food in people's freezers started to thaw, Horter saw barbecues come out and many people in the neighbourhood sharing meals. "We had essentially a community barbecue that lasted for a week. Everybody was coming together and helping each other out, and it was really a community builder." A few years after the quake, Horter moved to Vancouver and found himself living in trendy Kitsilano, a neighbourhood of cafés, condos, and yoga studios. According to crime statistics, he had ended up in a safer community. And yet he wondered if his new home was somehow less secure, because people there lived more isolated, solitary lives. West Oakland "was the best community I ever lived in," he says. "It was the poorest community, but people actually looked out for each other."

A sense of community can be crucial, and developing emergency plans with neighbours can save lives. But, Robert Gifford cautions, a strong attachment to place is problematic if it prevents people from leaving places where they really shouldn't stay. Of course, not everyone can move. Millions of impoverished people in the low-lying flood plains of Bangladesh, for instance, have little choice but to stay put. In the developed world, however, people who live on flood plains and tsunami inundation zones face mounting pressure to move, as do people living where wildfires or rising sea levels threaten their homes.

In 2014 a passionate debate followed Oregon State University's announcement of a new marine studies building in Newport, right in the tsunami inundation zone, where the university's Hatfield Marine Science Center was built more than fifty years earlier on a narrow spit of land across the bay from the city. The drab exterior offered few hints of the important research that took place inside. With growing concern about climate change, ocean acidification, and falling fish stocks, the university decided to build a new $50-million building right next to the old one, even though a few different sites were considered, including two uphill and out of the tsunami zone.

The backlash to the decision was loud and clear, and it came from people who were especially difficult to ignore. The state geologist at the time, Vicki McConnell, urged the university president to reconsider. Geological records show tsunami waves as high as thirteen metres crashed ashore in the area in the past, she pointed out, and the Hatfield Center is no higher than six metres above sea level. "I know you are not willing to put even one, much less 500, students and researchers in peril every day," she wrote. She cited Oregon's 1999 law prohibiting the construction of any new buildings designed to accommodate 501 people or more in a tsunami inundation zone, noting the hundred-thousand-square-foot building had a maximum occupancy of five hundred. At least a dozen faculty members echoed her concerns, warning the new facility could "threaten lives, damage buildings and hobble the research capacity of this flagship institute."

University officials insisted the location was the best site for the new facility because of the need to pump nearly a million gallons of seawater from the bay into laboratories every day. Pumping that water uphill would be prohibitively expensive, they argued. And despite the building's official capacity, only rarely would more than three hundred people be in the building at one time. The new building would be built to the highest seismic standards and able to sustain a magnitude-9 earthquake. The building would be attached to a series of steel-reinforced concrete pilings sunk deep into the sandy soil. That sandy land is likely to liquefy in a giant subduction earthquake, but the pilings are designed to remain standing and support the roof, which would act as a vertical tsunami evacuation tower, similar to the elementary school in Ocosta, Washington. University officials also pointed to the new student housing facilities that would be built uphill, above the tsunami inundation zone, and noted that Safe Haven Hill, Newport's designated tsunami evacuation site, is only a twelve-minute walk from the Hatfield Center — scientists estimate it would take thirty minutes after a major subduction earthquake before a tsunami slammed into Newport.

Depending on who you ask, Oregon State University should be applauded for including the most stringent safety measures available in its new building, or condemned for putting that building in the path of a future tsunami. Only when the tsunami strikes will anyone know if the university made a wise decision.

The truth is none of us can be sure how our homes and cities will respond—or how we will. We can't prepare for every possible outcome, even if we wanted to. But, Robert Gifford says, "This is not an event you can do nothing about. You can't stop the earthquake from happening. You *can* stop the earthquake from killing you."

Epilogue

LIVING WITH THE RISK

As a journalist, I've spent nearly two decades interviewing hundreds of geologists, seismologists, geophysicists, oceanographers, volcanologists, engineers, emergency planners, survivors, and many more about earthquakes. Yet in all that time, I've done little to prepare. I choose not to send my kids to a school with unreinforced masonry walls, and we didn't buy a house in a tsunami inundation zone, but I haven't made personal plans or stocked up on supplies. Fortunately for us, my wife bought an orange emergency backpack that's full of first-aid supplies and a few fifteen-litre water carriers, and she's made sure our tents, sleeping bags, and camping stove are accessible in our backyard shed. But the supplies have strayed and dwindled over the course of a few summer holidays, and I'm embarrassed to admit that three years after I started writing this book about earthquakes, I was no more prepared than when I began. I decided to finally get started in earnest.

I began with a relatively cheap and simple project. The fifty-gallon hot-water tank in my basement is incredibly heavy when full and in serious shaking could easily tip over, spraying scalding hot water and flooding the basement floor. I went to my local hardware store and paid a little more than $20 for a pair of galvanized steel water-heater straps that are designed to keep tanks like mine standing upright in a serious quake. (This can provide us with a valuable source of clean drinking water.) They took less than half an hour to install. If only all earthquake preparations were so easy! After a few minutes of admiring my handiwork, I looked up at where the wood post now anchoring the tank met the horizontal wood beam above it. With just a few nails holding this critical junction together, the two massive timbers could come apart in strong shaking, letting the house collapse. I seized the moment and cycled back to the hardware store to buy a handful of T-shaped galvanized-steel plates and nailed them to the post and beam. Before long, I'd plucked the low-hanging seismic fruit. I called a structural engineer to help me with the harder stuff.

I've interviewed Graham Taylor, who showed me the giant shake table at the University of British Columbia, several times over the years. When I called this time, Taylor was busy working for the British Columbia government on the prioritized post-earthquake response assessment system that will help engineers determine whether key public buildings like hospitals and schools are safe to occupy after a major earthquake. Taylor hopes that studying the design of each building and the type of soil it sits on, and installing accelerometers to record the force of the shaking in an earthquake, will give engineers enough information to get a jump-start on post-earthquake assessment so key buildings can reopen quickly and safely.

We met on a busy weekday afternoon, with the chaos of kids and the dog circling us, and sat at my kitchen table to discuss what he would do. Helping people with the seismic remediation of their homes, he says, has offered him interesting insights into human nature and the common motivations that lead people to prepare. (Women, he says, call him far more often than men.) Many of Taylor's clients are delighted and have gone ahead with renovations right away. Others struggle with the ramifications of what might happen after a major earthquake, even if their house is still standing. "The thing that has floored a lot of people—and most people have had to put it in their back pocket because they couldn't deal with it—is the social issue, the mayhem that's going to come. Not necessarily that you have to be self-reliant, but that there's going to be no police protection. What if you've got a person on the block that's not very nice, and you have to deal with them? How are you going to deal with them? I don't think any of us are prepared to follow that very far." One couple decided it was easier to move away from the earthquake risk than address it directly.

Most people stay, and Taylor is adamant that renovating our houses is the best thing that those of us in a seismic zone can do. While death and injury are serious concerns in a major earthquake, Taylor points out we're more likely to be left homeless. He describes a seismic retrofit as a form of self-insurance that gives people like me a much better chance of staying in our homes.

My house is worth saving for its own sake. It's clad from top to bottom in cedar shingles that have weathered more than one hundred windy winters and sunny summers. The large rectangular windows on the main floor let in lots of light, and attractive white muntins divide the panes of the smaller windows upstairs. The front hallway and the dining room still have six-foot-high Douglas fir wainscotting. Though my family has only lived in it for seven years, this old house is our home. As Taylor and I went down into the basement, it dawned on me how much I wanted to protect it.

The bedrock beneath the house is visible in a few spots. "You've got that rock going for you," Taylor observed. But a lot of weight is perched on top of the basement. The foundation is a rectangle consisting of the concrete floor and four waist-high concrete walls. Sandwiched between those walls and the weight of the house are four shorter pony walls. They're built of two-inch-by-four-inch wood studs held together with thin boards. If the earth moves the foundation and inertia keeps the upper part of the house in place, any one of the pony walls could be the straw that breaks the camel's back. "The basement is pulling the whole two storeys with it," Taylor noted. "That's a real concern as the two storeys are not going to move, but the foundation moves with the ground."

Taylor left, promising to return in a few weeks with a report telling me how to make my house stronger, and I headed out to a store called Total Prepare. The squat rectangular building sits just a stone's throw from the highway that leads to the ferry terminal and features a giant all-caps sign in the window: EARTHQUAKE KITS. Inside, Zenia Platten introduced herself as a jack-of-all-trades and content creator. She's worked at the store for a few years and designs a lot of their earthquake kits, putting together the seemingly endless combinations of medical supplies, toiletries, rescue tools, freeze-dried food, cooking supplies, and just about anything else.

Online orders from all over Canada and beyond keep Total Prepare busy. Platten has sold emergency supplies to customers worried about solar flares, a man who was preparing for unemployment, and a mine manager who expected environmental protestors would block him in at the mine site. She's had those who want to prepare for the Rapture, and also preppers, who are readying for a variety of imminent catastrophes, from natural disasters to widespread social disruption. "Ninety per cent of the time they're wearing camo, and they know exactly what they need. They know more about the stuff than we do!"

Most of the online customers who live east of the Rockies want to prepare for blizzards, extended power outages, or tornadoes. In British Columbia, most want to get ready for earthquakes and tsunamis. "You almost never hear of anything else here," Platten said. During its first decade in business, Total Prepare saw a huge rush of customers every time a big earthquake made international headlines. Customers also come in droves after a local earthquake makes itself felt. Just before midnight on New Year's Eve, 2015, a small undersea earthquake between Vancouver and Victoria spooked a lot of people, including me. A long line of people emptied Total Prepare's shelves the next day.

People who come to buy emergency supplies already own first-aid kits and camping gear, Platten said, and as a result, they already have most of what they need. The most popular earthquake supplies at this store are kits of freeze-dried food in easily transportable watertight pails. The food will keep for twenty years. A seven-gallon pail can feed one person for a month or a family of four for a week and costs $250, roughly what a person or a family would spend on groceries for the same period.

Clean drinking water is another matter. Many cities have lost water supply for days or even weeks when earthquakes crack water mains. Most of us take water for granted, and it is staggering how much we consume. The average North American uses more than three hundred litres of water a day. No doubt we could do with less, as most of the world's people do, especially as most of that water flows through washing machines, dishwashers, and toilets. I figured my family will need at least twenty litres a day. But what if our water supply was disrupted for longer than a week? A 2018 study suggested Seattle might lose water pressure within twenty-four hours of a major quake and need *two months* to restore full service. The water in our 180-litre hot-water tank wouldn't be enough. I spent $160 on a gravity-fed water purification system that can remove 99.99 percent of protozoa, 99.999 percent of viruses, and 99.9999 percent of bacteria from 18,000 litres of water, and later I stopped by a hardware store to pick up three rainwater collection barrels that can store 560 litres.

Over the next few weeks, I assembled some of the essential items that we didn't have in our emergency kit: a manual can opener, some extra cash, and copies of our birth certificates and passports. I packed clothes for each of us, which included several pristine shirts and pants bought for my sons by their grandparents (they'll be much better dressed after a major earthquake than on any other day, except perhaps Christmas). I also bought a new bag of dog food for Toby, our lanky German shepherd–coonhound cross. The preparations made me feel a bit better, but until I know our house is relatively safe, I won't consider myself truly prepared. If a disaster leaves us homeless, we'll have a whole new set of challenges.

Graham Taylor's return visit brought both good news and bad. The good news is that our house can be made a lot safer. The bad news is that it is at considerable risk. Taylor calculates it could suffer serious damage if the ground under it moves sideways with a force equivalent to 15 percent of gravitational acceleration (15%g). That's its resilience threshold. At 25%g the house might collapse or be so heavily damaged that it could kill us. That's its life-safety threshold. Houses built to the current British Columbia building code should have resilience thresholds of 24%g and life-safety thresholds of 43%g. If we strengthen our house, Taylor estimates it will have a resilience threshold of 35%g and a life-safety threshold of 45%g.

Of course, even harder shaking could hit the house. Accelerometers have recorded higher ground force acceleration in several earthquakes around the world, including an astonishing 300%g in New Zealand on the concrete floor of a farm shed directly above one of the more than twenty faults that ruptured in the magnitude-7.8 Kaikoura earthquake. But the next major earthquake to hit us will most likely come from the offshore subduction zone, which means we won't feel the full force of the shaking, and we can expect considerably lower peak ground acceleration, thanks to the bedrock under our house.

I need to nail plywood to the vertical wall studs on the four-foot-high basement walls. That will transfer the primary pressure from the basement up to the main floor walls, which are three metres tall and therefore better able to absorb the shearing movement between the moving ground and the bulk of the house. "It's something that's achievable," Taylor reassured me. "And if you're able to do it yourself, so much the better." He would specify the measurements and nailing patterns and said I can nail the plywood on the inside or the outside, depending on whether I want to remove the exterior siding or the interior drywall. He estimated hiring a professional to do the work will cost between $15,000 and $20,000. That's cheaper than tearing down post-quake wreckage and building new, but living in one of North America's most expensive real estate markets means Becky and I have a hefty mortgage. I decided to do the work myself, bit by bit over the next few years. Taylor will draw up basic plans and inspect my work at a few crucial stages. When I'm finished, he'll sign a letter attesting to the work that's been done and giving the house a new safety rating. In the meantime, he recommended I install an accelerometer in the basement. At first I wondered why I'd pay money to measure the shaking under my house. What good will that do me before the earthquake? But after an earthquake, comparing a precise measurement of exactly how much the ground under my house shook to Taylor's assessment will give me a much better idea of whether my house had sustained serious, unseen damage.

Taylor has already installed these instruments in pilot projects in schools, fire halls, and government buildings. He's trying to convince small groups of neighbours to sign up together and lease a single accelerometer, which would be installed in one of their basements. If a group of five or six households came together, they could have this service for about $60 a year each. I invited twenty neighbours to club together to pay for a four-year connection to an accelerometer in my basement. Three decided to join me.

And what about the rest of us, and all of our buildings? The truth is thousands of houses, apartments, offices, towers, factories, warehouses, bridges, dams, overpasses, and tunnels remain vulnerable. Some owners will replace or strengthen them, some communities will mandate more repairs, and some will combine seismic work with energy retrofit programs that are part of the effort to fight climate change. It's unlikely all of them will be strengthened before the next big earthquake strikes a large North American city, but when it does I hope as many of these vulnerable structures as possible have either been replaced or strengthened. And if it feels like the next big earthquake is a long way off, consider that more than one hundred magnitude-6 or greater earthquakes have rumbled around the world in the year it's taken to edit this book.

Now that I'm finished writing, I will start prying off the old cedar shakes from the exterior basement walls of my house and start nailing new plywood to the old wall studs. I plan to fix two sides this year and tackle the other two next year. Will I finish before the next Big One hits? I certainly hope so.

Acknowledgements

Journalists typically know a little about a lot of different things, and as a result we often find it humbling to meet experts with deep wells of knowledge in individual subjects. That was certainly the case for me when I interviewed the many geologists, seismologists, oceanographers, structural engineers, emergency planners, and other experts who helped me write this book. I have listed all of the people who spoke to me directly in Sources, but I want to make special mention here of John Cassidy, at the Geological Survey of Canada, who is unfailingly helpful to journalists in British Columbia and beyond. I have certainly benefited from both his expertise and his willingness to answer questions. I urge anyone who is interested in earthquakes to follow John on Twitter: @earthquakeguy. I'm also grateful to his colleague Honn Kao, who discussed with me not only the geological aspects of earthquakes but some of the social aspects as well. I've also benefited from the knowledge and patience of John Adams, Alison Bird, Taimi Mulder, and other professionals at the Geological Survey of Canada. I am similarly indebted to various scientists at the University of Victoria's Ocean Networks Canada, which has conducted extensive underwater research, and in particular ONC president Kate Moran.

I've been equally reliant on engineers who have spent decades making buildings and other infrastructure safer. I've interviewed many, and I am hugely indebted to Graham Taylor, who has given me much of his time, as well as Tuna Onur, who answered many questions and, at my request, even looked at an old cinder-block house once. I've also imposed on several emergency planners. Eric Holdeman in Seattle was extremely helpful, and Doug Dougherty (whose official job title was school superintendent but who arguably led a whole city to prepare for the Big One) was similarly accommodating when I visited Seaside, Oregon.

I'm especially grateful to the survivors of earthquakes who spoke to me about those terrifying moments. I know from firsthand experience that it is not easy to recount moments of trauma, so I appreciate that Marley Daviduk, Will Horter, Lynda Kaye, Claire Kelly, Anne Mullens, Jim Reimer, Paula Romagosa, Ellen Saenger, Carisa Webster, Haley Westra, Keith Vass, Sarah Murray, and Deborah Wilson were willing to speak to me about their terrifying ordeals.

I'm indebted to many of my journalist colleagues who have helped me tell many of these stories on the radio over the years, and once again I want to thank Deborah Wilson specifically. After living through the Mexico quake of 1985, Debbie turned her experience into action. She was the first journalist to open my eyes to the specific threats in Victoria, just as she informed many thousands of other people in this city through the stories she wrote and produced.

This book really took shape when I enrolled at the University of King's College in Halifax for the limited-residency master of fine arts program. I learned a great deal from my fellow students, the excellent professors, and my two writing mentors, Ken McGoogan and David Hayes. I'm grateful to the BC Arts Council for providing me with a scholarship that funded part of my studies and the travel necessary to write this book.

I was extremely lucky to meet my literary agent, Chris Bucci, when visiting New York. He worked diligently with me to craft a proposal, and when I spoke to Matthew Halliday at Goose Lane Editions, I had a very good feeling about Canada's oldest independent publisher. That impression has grown stronger as I've worked with his colleagues Alan Sheppard and Julie Scriver. I count myself lucky to have worked with the excellent editor Jill Ainsley, who has done a fine job editing a sometimes unwieldy manuscript, and to copy editor Caroline Skelton for bringing it to its finished form.

Finally, I would like to thank my family. My three sons have reminded me on many occasions to stop worrying about the future and live in the moment, as the cliché goes. In contrast my mother, Betty, and my sister, Gillian, have reminded me that we can all do more to keep each other safe and that we must protect the most vulnerable among us. Above all I'm grateful to my wife, Becky, who gave me the time, support, and understanding required to write this book.

Sources

Interviews

John Adams, Calvin Campbell, John Cassidy, Divya Chandrasekhar, Marley Daviduk, David Dooley, Doug Dougherty, Robert Gifford, Ronald Hamburger, Eric Holdeman, Will Horter, Steven Jaume, Jeanne Johnson, Honn Kao, Claire Kelly, Alison Macfarlane, Charles Mergeurian, Seth Moran, Anne Mullens, Marie-José Nollet, Zenia Platten, Pierre Poirier, Jim Reimer, Paula Romagosa, Christie Rowe, Murat Saatcioglu, Julian Sharpe, Lynn R. Sykes, Graham Taylor, Carisa Webster, Haley Westra, Jim Wilkinson, Deborah Wilson, and Ivan Wong.

Newspapers and News Sites

ABC, www.abc.net.au
Associated Press, www.apnews.com
BBC News, www.bbc.com/news
British Colonist, www.britishcolonist.ca
The Bulletin (Bend, OR)
Buzzfeed, www.buzzfeednews.com
CBC News, www.cbc.ca/news
CBS News, www.cbsnews.com
Chronicling America: Historic American Newspapers, https://
    chroniclingamerica.loc.gov
The Columbian (Vancouver, WA)
Corvallis Gazette-Times
Dallas Morning News
Deseret News

Free Press (St. John's, NL)
Georgia Straight
The Guardian
Halifax Chronicle Herald
Japan Times
Los Angeles Times
Montreal Gazette
National Post
New York Times
New Zealand Herald
News Tribune (Tacoma, WA)
Peruvian Times
The Province (Vancouver, BC)
Radio New Zealand, www.radionz.co.nz
Register Guard (Eugene, OR)
Reuters, www.reuters.com
Salem Statesman Journal
Salem Weekly News
Salt Lake Tribune
San Francisco Chronicle
Savannah Morning News
Seattle Times
South China Morning Post
Southern Gazette
St. Louis Post-Dispatch
Stuff, www.stuff.co.nz
Sydney Morning Herald
The Telegraph
US News and World Report
USA Today
Vancouver Sun
Washington Evening Star

Websites
Alaska Earthquake Center, www.earthquake.alaska.edu
CalTrans, www.dot.ca.gov
Central Tower, www.centraltowersf.com
Dictionary of Canadian Biography, www.biographi.ca/en
Digital Museums Canada, www.digitalmuseums.ca

Disaster History, www.disasterhistory.org

The Earth Institute, Columbia University, www.earth.columbia.edu

GeoNet, www.geonet.org.nz

GNS Science, www.gns.cri.nz

Great Shakeout, www.shakeout.org

The Museum of the City of San Francisco, www.sfmuseum.net

National Geographic, www.nationalgeographic.com

National Museum of Natural History, www.naturalhistory.si.edu

National Oceanic and Atmospheric Administration, www.noaa.gov

National Park Service, www.nps.gov

Natural Resources Canada, www.nrcan.gc.ca/home

New Zealand History, https://nzhistory.govt.nz

Oregon Department of Geology and Mineral Industries, www
.oregongeology.org

Oregon State University Volcano World, http://volcano.oregonstate.edu

Pacific Northwest Seismic Network, https://pnsn.org

San Diego State University Department of Geological Sciences, https://
geology.sdsu.edu

Science Daily, www.sciencedaily.com

The Skyscraper Museum, https://skyscraper.org

South Carolina Earthquake Education and Preparedness, https://
scearthquakes.cofc.edu

United States Geological Survey, www.usgs.gov

University of Southern California Tsunami Research Center, www
.tsunamiresearchcenter.com

Washington State Department of Transportation, www.wsdot.wa.gov

Reports and Web Documents

Adams, John, and Michael Staveley. *Historical Seismicity of Newfoundland.* Ottawa: Earth Physics Branch Open File No. 85-22, Seismological Service of Canada, 1985.

Ashland, Francis X. *Reconnaissance of the Draper Heights Landslide and Other Possible Earthquake-Induced, Shallow, Disrupted Soil and Rock Slides in Draper, Utah.* Utah Geological Survey, 2008.

Atwater, Brian F., Satoko Musumi-Rokkaku, Kenji Satake, Yoshinobu Tsuji, Kazue Ueda, and David K. Yamaguchi. *The Orphan Tsunami of 1700: Japanese Clues to a Parent Earthquake in North America.* US Geological Survey Professional Paper 1707, 2005.

Canterbury Earthquakes Royal Commission Final Report, Vols. 1-7, 2012.

Centre for Research on the Epidemiology of Disasters. *The Human Cost of Natural Disasters: A Global Perspective*. Brussels, 2015.

City of Richmond, BC. *Tsunamis and Richmond*. www.richmond.ca/safety /prepare/city/hazards/tsunamis/tsunamistudy.htm.

Coronial Services of New Zealand. *Canterbury Earthquake CTV Building Inquiry*. March 27, 2014.

Earthquake Engineering Research Institute, Utah Chapter. *Scenario for a Magnitude 7.0 Earthquake on the Wasatch Fault–Salt Lake City Segment*. June 4, 2015.

Emergency Management Division, Washington State. *Understanding Tsunami Hazards in the State of Washington: How Vulnerable is the City of Westport to Tsunamis?* 2013.

Fukushima Nuclear Accident Independent Investigation Commission. *The Official Report of the Fukushima Nuclear Accident Independent Investigation Commission: Executive Summary*. Tokyo: The National Diet of Japan, 2012.

González, Frank I., compiler. *Puget Sound Tsunami Sources: 2002 Workshop Report*. Washington: National Oceanic and Atmospheric Administration, 2003.

Head, Lloyd. "One Boy's Experience: A Member of the Roosevelt Boys' Club Writes of His Experience During and After the Great Earthquake." Originally published in *Our Junior Citizens* (July 28, 1906). Museum of the City of San Francisco, www.sfmueum.net/1906 /ew7.html.

Hyland, Clark and Ashley Smith. *CTV Building Collapse Investigation for the Department of Building and Housing, Part 1*. Hyland Consultants, 2012.

Hyland, Michael D. "How Active are the End Segments of the Wasatch Fault Zone? New Information from Geologic Mapping and Scarp Studies." *Utah Geological Survey Notes* 39, no. 1 (January 2007).

Kayden, Robert and Walter A. Barnhardt, "Seismic Stability of the Duwamish River Delta, Seattle, Washington." USGS professional paper 1661-E, 2007.

National Weather Service. "Flood History of Mississippi." www.weather .gov/media/jan/JAN/Hydro/Flood_History_MS.pdf.

Renteria, Henry. *British Columbia Earthquake Preparedness: Consultation Report*. Victoria: Government of British Columbia, 2014.

Swan, F.H., David P. Schwartz, Kathryn L. Hanson, Peter L. Knuepfer, and Lloyd S. Cluff. *Study of Earthquake Recurrence Intervals on the Wasatch Fault at the Kaysville Site, Utah*. San Francisco: Woodward-Clyde Consultants, 1979.

Swiss Re Institute. *Earthquake Risk in Eastern Canada: Mind the Shakes.* Zurich: Swiss Re Institute, 2017.

Tantala, Michael, Guy Nordenson, George Deodatis, Klaus Jacob, Bruce Swiren, Michael Augustyniak, Andrea Dargush, MaryAnn Marrocolo, and Daniel O'Brien. *Earthquake Risks and Mitigation in the New York/New Jersey/Connecticut Region, 1999-2003.* New York: NYCEM, 2003.

US Geological Survey. *New Madrid Earthquake Sequence: Personal Accounts from the 1811–1812 New Madrid Earthquakes.* USGS GIP 118, December 2011-February 2012.

———. *The Mississippi Valley: "Whole Lotta Shakin' Goin' On."* USGS fact-sheet 168-95, 1995.

———. *Progress Toward a Safer Future Since the 1989 Loma Prieta Earthquake.* USGS fact sheet 151-99, 1999.

Ventura, Carlos, Armin Bebamzadeh, and Michael Fairhurst. "City-wide Seismic Vulnerability Assessment of the City of Victoria." City of Victoria: May 2, 2017.

Books, Articles, and Conference Papers

Adams, John. "Paleoseismicity of the Cascadia Subduction Zone: Evidence from the Turbidites off the Oregon-Washington Margin." *Tectonics* 9, no. 4 (August 1990): 569-83.

Aggarwal, Yash P., and Lynn R. Sykes. "Earthquakes, Faults, and Nuclear Power Plants in Southern New York and Northern New Jersey." *Science* 200, no. 4340 (April 28, 1978): 425-29.

Barstow, Erin. "Fort Bragg Barracks Receives Pioneering Force Protection Retrofit." *Public Works Digest* XXI, no. 3 (May-June 2009): 28.

Benyaminov, Zoya Susan, Merins Sadiku, and Mishka Stueber. "Re-assessing the New York City Seismic Design Building Code." *Journal of Environment and Ecology* 8, no. 1 (2017): 152-65.

Berry, Lynn. "Le ciel et la terre nous ont parlé: Comment les missionnaires du Canada française de l'époque coloniale interprétènt le tremblement de terre de 1663." *Revue d'Histoire de l'Amerique Française* 60, nos. 1-2 (2006): 11-35.

Boas, Franz. "Traditions of the Tillamook Indians." *Journal of American Folklore* 11, no. 40 (January-March 1898): 23-38.

Bonowitz, David. *The Dilemma of Existing Buildings: Private Property, Public Risk.* (San Francisco: SPUR, 2009).

Brand, David. "Tree-ring Study Enables Researchers to Link Massive American Earthquake to Japanese Tsunami in January 1700" *UW News* (October 29, 1997).

Breu, Giovanni and Sue Ellen Jares. "Geologist's Survivors Defend His Memory After the Latest Mount St. Helens Fallout: A Film Charging US Cover-up." *People* (March 30, 1981).

Cherniawsky, Josef, Kelin Wang, and Roy Walters. "Predicting Tsunami Waves and Currents on the West Coast of Canada: A Case Study for Ucluelet" (Paper presented at PICES annual meeting, Hiroshima, Japan, October 2012).

Côté, Richard N. *City of Heroes: The Great Charleston Earthquake of 1886* (Mt. Pleasant, SC: Corinthian Books, 2006).

Crandell, Dwight Raymond and Donal Ray Mullineaux. "Potential Hazards from Future Eruptions of Mount St. Helens Volcano, Washington." *USGS Bulletin* 1383-C (1978).

De Feo, Robert J. "Northridge Meadows Apartment Collapse." *Fire Engineering* (August 1, 1994).

Doughton, Sandi. *Full-Rip 9.0: The Next Big Earthquake in the Pacific Northwest* (Seattle: Sasquatch Books, 2013).

Ebel, John E. *New England Earthquakes: The Surprising History of Seismic Activity in the Northeast* (Guilford, CT: Globe Pequot, 2019).

El Sabbagh, Amid. "Seismic Risk Assessment of Unreinforced Masonry Buildings Using Fuzzy Based Techniques for the Regional Seismic Risk Assessment of Ottawa, Ontario" (master's thesis, University of Ottawa, 2014).

Findley, Rowe. "Mountain with a Death Wish." *National Geographic* (January 1981).

Finn, W.D. Liam, Carlos E. Ventura, and Norman D. Schuster. "Ground Motions During the 1994 Northridge Earthquake." *Canadian Journal of Civil Engineering* 22, no. 2 (2011): 300-15.

Fountain, Henry. *The Great Quake: How the Biggest Earthquake in North America Changed Our Understanding of the Planet* (New York: Crown, 2017.)

Gang, Qian. *The Great China Earthquake* (Beijing: Foreign Languages Press, 1989.)

Geller, Robert J., David D. Jackson, Yan Y. Kagan, and Francesco Mulargia. "Earthquakes Cannot Be Predicted." *Science* 275, no. 5306 (March 14, 1997): 1616-17.

"God, I Want to Live!" *Time* (June 2, 1980).

Goldfinger, Chris. "Deep-water Turbidites as Holocene Earthquake Proxies." *Annals of Geophysics* 46, no. 5 (October 2003): 1169-94.

Griggs, Gary. "The First Ocean Floor Evidence of Great Cascadia Quakes." *Eos* 92, no. 39 (September 2011): 325-26.

Gross, Ashley. "Tacoma Quake Survivor Remains Grateful to the Boy Who Died Saving His Life 67 Years Ago." KNKX (September 7, 2019), http://knkx.org/post/tacoma-quake-survivor-remains-grateful-to-boy-who-died-saving-his-life-67-years-ago.

Gunes, O. "Turkey's Grand Challenge: Disaster-proof Building Inventory Within 20 Years." *Case Studies in Contruction Materials* 2 (June 2015): 18-34.

Hamburger, Ronald O. and James O. Malley. "Revisting Earthquake Lessons: Welded Steel Moment Resisting Connections." *SEAOC News* (September 22, 2018), www.seaoc.org/news.

Heaton, Thomas H. and Parke D. Snavely, Jr. "Possible Tsunami Along the Northwestern Coast of the United States Inferred from Indian Traditions." *Bulletin of the Seismological Society of America* 75, no. 5 (October 1985): 1455-60.

Henderson, Bonnie. *The Next Tsunami: Living on a Restless Coast* (Corvallis, OR: OSU Press, 2014.)

Hunter, Dana. "Dedication: The Geologists Who Died at Mount St. Helens." *Scientific American* (May 30, 2012).

Jackson, Brett. "Replacing Oakland's Cypress Freeway." *Public Roads* 61, no. 5 (March/April 1998): 30-35.

James, William. *Memories and Studies* (New York: Longmans, Green, 1912.)

Jennings, Paul C., ed. *Engineering Features of the San Fernando Earthquake of February 9, 1971.* Pasadena, CA: California Institute of Technology, 1971.

Joffe, Helene. "Cultural Barriers to Earthquake Preparedness." *Risk Management* 59, no. 5 (2012): 20-25.

Kafka, Alan. "Faults and Earthquakes in the Greater NY City Area: Reflections at the Intersection of Science, the Media, and the Public." *Earthquakes and Related Matters* (blog), https://akafka.wordpress.com.

Leblanc, Gabriel. "A Closer Look at the September 16, 1732, Montreal Earthquake." *Canadian Journal of Earth Science* 18 (1981): 539-50.

Ludwin, Ruth S., Robert Dennis, Deborah Carver, Alan D. McMillan, Robert Losey, John Clague, Chris Jonientz-Trisler, Janine Bowechop, Jacilee Wray, and Karen James. "Dating the 1700 Cascadia Earthquake: Great Coastal Earthquakes in Native Stories." *Seismological Research Letters* 76, no. 2 (March 2005): 140-48.

Lyles, James Stevenson. "Investigating Seismic Successes and Failures in 1886 Charleston" (master's thesis, Clemson University, 2018).

Lyman, Edwin, Michael Schoeppner, and Frank von Hippel. "Nuclear Safety Regulation in the Post-Fukushima Era: Flawed Analyses Underlie Lax US Regulation of Spent Fuel." *Science* 356, no. 6340 (May 26, 2017): 808-09.

Miles, Scott B. and Brian Gouran. "U.S. Earthquake Policy Activity and Coverage." *Earthquake Spectra* 32, no. 1 (February 2016): 633-49.

Newcomb, Tim. "Digging the World's Widest Tunnel Under Downtown Seattle." *Popular Mechanics* (August 30, 2012).

Nuttli, Otto W. "Contemporary Newspaper Accounts of Mississippi Valley Earthquakes of 1811-1812." Department of Earth and Atmospheric Sciences, Saint Louis University, St. Louis, MO, www.eas.slu.edu /eqc_history/OWNuttli/Nuttli.1973/nuttli-73-app.html.

Pratt, Sara E. "March 27, 1964: The Good Friday Alaska Earthquake and Tsunamis." *Earth* 59, no. 3 (February 2014): 54.

Roeloffs, E. and J. Langbein. "The Earthquake Prediction Experiment at Parkfield, California." *Reviews of Geophysics* 32, no. 3 (1994): 315-36.

Ruffman, Alan and Violette Hann. "The Newfoundland Tsunami of November 18, 1929: An Examination of the Twenty-eight Deaths of the 'South Coast Disaster.'" *Newfoundland and Labrador Studies* 21, no. 1 (2006): 1719-26.

Rusch, Elizabeth. "The Great Midwest Earthquake of 1811." *Smithsonian* magazine (December 2011).

Scawthorn, C., T.D. O'Rourke, and F.T. Blackburn. "The 1906 San Francisco Earthquake and Fire—Enduring Lessons for Fire Protection and Water Supply." *Earthquake Spectra* 22, no. 2 (April 2006): S135-58.

Schulz, Kathryn. "The Really Small Ones." *New Yorker* (November 4, 2016).

Slatta, Richard W. *The Mythical West: An Encyclopedia of Legend, Lore, and Popular Culture* (Santa Barbara, CA: ABC-Clio, 2001).

Statake, Kenji, Kunihiko Shimazaki, Yoshinobu Tsuji, and Kazue Ueda. "Time and Size of a Giant Earthquake in Cascadia Inferred from Japanese Tsunami Records of January 1700." *Nature* 379 (January 1996): 246-49.

Suzuki, Wataru, Shin Aoi, Haruko Sekiguchi, and Takashi Kunugi. "Source Rupture Process of the Tohoku Oki Earthquake Derived from the Strong Motion Records." (Paper presented at the 15th World

Conference on Earthquake Engineering, Lisbon, Portugal, September 2012).

Sykes, Lynn R., John G. Armbruster, Won-Young Kim, and Leonardo Seeber. "Observations and Tectonic Setting of Historic and Instrumentally Located Earthquakes in the Greater New York City –Philadelphia Area." *Bulletin of the Seismological Society of America* 98, no. 4 (August 2008): 1696-1719.

Ten Brink, Uri. "The Puerto Rico Trench: Implications for Plate Tectonics and Earthquake and Tsunami Hazards." NOAA Ocean Explorer, https://oceanexplorer.noaa.gov/explorations/03/trench/trench/trench .html.

Vancouver, George. *A Voyage of Discovery to the North Pacific Ocean and Round the World*, Vol. 2 (London: G.G. and J. Robinson, 1798).

Wang, Kelin, Qi-Fu Chen, Shihong Sun, and Andong Wang. "Predicting the 1975 Haicheng Earthquake." *Bulletin of the Seismological Society of America* 96, no. 3 (June 2006): 757-95.

Ward, Steven N. and Simon Day. "Cumbre Vieja Volcano: Potential Collapse and Tsunami at La Palma, Canary Islands." *Geophysical Research Letters* 28, no. 17 (2001): 3397-3400.

Yeats, Robert S. *Living with Earthquakes in the Pacific Northwest: A Survivor's Guide*. 2nd ed. (Corvallis, OR: OSU Press, 2004).

Zalzal, Kate S. "August 31, 1886: Magnitude-7 Earthquake Rocks Charleston, South Carolina." *Earth* 62, no. 8 (August 2017): 57.

Zentner, Nick. "Mt. Rainier's Osceola Mudflow." *Nick on the Rocks* season 1, episode 4, PBS, December 28, 2017, www.pbs.org/video/nick-rocks -mt-rainiers-osceola/mudflow/.

Gregor Craigie is one of Canada's most experienced journalists. He is the current host of CBC's *On the Island* in Victoria, British Columbia. His interest in earthquakes was sparked during his work as a legislative correspondent for CBC Television, when he began studying the seismically vulnerable BC legislature. Since then, he has been in regular contact with scientists, engineers, and other earthquake experts.

Craigie has also worked as an international reporter for CBS Radio; a producer for CBC Radio's *The Current*; and a journalist for the BBC World Service, where he produced radio documentaries and read the news to millions of American listeners of *The World* on Public Radio International. He has travelled to dozens of countries in his work as a journalist. *On Borrowed Time* is his first book.

Photo by Rebecca Craigie